Surviving and thriving as a Junior Lawyer

By Piper McKenzie

Table of Contents

Introduction

Congratulations on graduating from law school! Hopefully you have had an enlightening 3-5 years in academia. You have read higher court judgements, have considered great questions of public and international law, and have examined the law through the prism of legal theory, feminism, and social theory. Unfortunately, you now actually have to get a job and pay for your law degree.

This book is aimed at assisting recently graduated law students in navigating life as a junior lawyer. It is written primarily from the perspective of a junior commercial lawyer from a common-law jurisdiction, being the USA, United Kingdom, Canada, Australia, Hong Kong and Singapore. While life as a junior lawyer varies depending on your jurisdiction, the challenges of working in a commercial law firm—managing partner and client expectations—while still having a life are universal.

A common fallacy is that the only possible career path outside law school is practicing law. It is quite possible for people who have graduated with a law degree to go into clerking, academia, government work, business or any other area that fits their fancy. Private practice is not the only option open to you. However, this book is aimed as assisting those people who have chosen to start their careers in private practice.

Your author, who is writing under a pseudonym, graduated from law schools in Australia and the United States, worked in a top-tier BigLaw firm in banking and then litigation, before leaving to become a specialist trial lawyer who is often brought in by small law firms to handle trials. They (we are using the gender-neutral singular) enjoyed their time in BigLaw but got out when they wanted to, on their own terms to follow their dream. This book is a combination of their wisdom, and the wisdom of their peers, some of whom are now partners at top BigLaw firms, while others have left the law entirely.

Readers should absorb the key messages in the book, but don't treat them like gospel. Every lawyer is a little bit different and wants slightly different things out of law. The secret is in working out what you want out of your legal career (interesting work, a large pay-packet, decent hours etc.) and how to use your strengths (are you a legal genius, a people person, or an hour churning machine) to get there. Importantly:

- Unless you have done a clinic, practicing law is nothing like law school.
- Practicing law is scary, but you'll get used to it. Remember, practicing makes perfect!
- You don't have to be a slave to an evil partner/firm. You can create a legal career with limited hours and working with good people.
- If you want to get out of where you are working, get out!

Everybody who reads this book and goes into a law firm is a human being with hopes, dreams and desires. This book is about how to best make a success of your time as a junior lawyer. This will involve working long hours, irregular hours and undergoing times of great stress. The important thing to realize is that you are a young adult of considerable talents. You don't have to be a lawyer and if you discover that the legal life doesn't suit you, you shouldn't let your sunk costs keep you there.

This book is divided into two broad parts. Chapters 1 to 7 focus mostly on life in a large commercial law firm. While much of this material is relevant to lawyers in small generalist or boutique firms, some of it will not be. Chapters 8-9 deal with the specific issues relating to life in smaller law firms, both as a graduate and as an ex-Biglaw lawyer who may wish to make the transition.

Chapter 1 – What your BigLaw partners won't tell you

Congratulations on being accepted into the top law firm in your city. You know it has an excellent reputation. Its partners are some of the top experts in their field, and they work collegiately and professionally to assist the client. It is excellently resourced and well-managed, and spends a great deal of time developing its staff who are of course the future of the firm. You also know that you will be expected to work hard, and then play hard. You also know that most of the above is not entirely, if at all, true.

Lesson 1 – Law firms are like any other business.

BigLaw firms get a bad rep at times. They can be seen as soulless sweatshops, working lawyers to death while the partners at the top get rich, while pulling the ladder up behind them, making it harder and harder for those who come behind to become partner. The reality is that, in most firms, there are plenty of successful, hardworking, decent people, doing a stressful job and doing it well. For every difficult partner who sleeps with his secretary and yells at their juniors, there are three or four affable, flawed people who are doing a high-pressure job to the best of their ability. Partners are human too!

However, in my time in BigLaw I had a number of conversations with junior lawyers where the following was said:

- 'Did you see what our PPP is? I can't believe that we got stuck with a pay freeze?'
- 'I billed x last year, but only got paid y'
- 'Morale here is terrible, I can't believe that the partners let this happen.'
- 'The firm doesn't have the same sense of community that it did x years ago. Now it is just about profitability'.

The problem is that the junior lawyer is treating the firm like a family, or an entity where you are rewarded for the amount of work you do, or a firm in which morale is a good thing in itself. A law firm is a business, and as soon as you realize this you'll understand a lot more about the way the firm operates.

A BigLaw firm is optimized to maximize Profit Per Partner (PPP) (i.e. the total profit the firm makes divided by the number of partners who share in the profit). It may choose to make certain investments (e.g. overseas offices, training graduate lawyers) in the hope of future returns but everything comes back to PPP. It is what gets managing partners hired and fired, and what keeps the top-performing partners from leaving the firm. If a BigLaw firm stopped focusing on PPP it would lose a number of its 'rainmakers' (partners with large client bases) to other, more profitable firms, which would make it even less profitable, and so on. In essence, a firm is like a labor hire company. It buys labor in bulk (associates), adds value to them (support staff, partners) and then re-sells that labor, bit by bit, to its clients at a much higher rate.

What does this mean practically for the junior lawyer? I'll use the conversations set out above:

- 'Did you see what our PPP is? I can't believe that we got stuck with a pay freeze?'
- 'I billed x last year, but only got paid y'

Law firms are profit maximizers, which means that they charge as much as the market will bear. At the same time they also buy labor at what the market will bear, i.e. what they need to pay to attract talented junior lawyers and retain enough of them so that they have sufficient senior lawyers and partners coming through. Junior lawyers are therefore paid at their replacement value, not at the value that they produce for the firms. The fact that you billed 'x' last year doesn't mean that they will pay you more, rather they will still pay you what they calculate will keep you, or enough of you, from jumping to a rival firm. Equally, the fact that the firm implemented a pay freeze may have nothing to do with its PPP—if there are no other jobs for you to jump to, then why would the firm increase pay?

- 'Morale here is terrible, I can't believe that the partners let this happen.'

Morale is always 'terrible' at BigLaw firms. BigLaw firms are full of smart junior lawyers, who think they are underpaid, working long hours. They are supported by support staff who think the junior lawyers are massively overpaid and obnoxious. They all report to partners who are under pressure and have to supervise a new bunch of baby lawyers every year. While your individual partner may be a lovely human being, they do like their share of the firm's profits to be as large as possible. No firm has ever voted in a managing partner on a 'we'll pay above market rates and everyone will be happier policy' (as opposed to certain law firms that do pay above market compensation as part of a broader business strategy – such as Wachtell Lipton Rosen and Katz in New York)

- 'The firm doesn't have the same sense of community that it did x years ago. Now it is just about profitability'.

When you joined the firm as a summer associate you believed all the hype about the sense of community at the firm. You made some great friends as a summer associate and had great social events. You're now 5 years in, have seen a few pay freezes, acts of corporate backstabbing, have seen a bunch of your friends leave, and your remaining friends in the firm are in separate sections and you never see them. Of course you're going to bemoan the changing sense of community. The firm didn't change. You did.

In a lot of ways, junior lawyers get treated well in law firms compared to other white-collar jobs, let alone blue-collar jobs. You get summer associateships, regular social activities, team-building activities, your own offices (sometimes), support staff, bonuses (sometimes) and sometimes caring partner mentors. But never confuse the fact that the firm wants to attract and maintain talent with some inherent benevolence. The firm is a business. Expect no more and no less.

Lesson 2 – Being a Summer Associate has little to do with being a lawyer

Summer associateships are generally pretty awesome. You get to wear a suit and go to a big office downtown. There are great social activities, and you get to tag along with the heavy hitters to the big cases. You have a buddy who is generally pretty friendly to you, and may take you out to lunch and give you a few tips. You get to do interesting research assignments and do some work on a pro bono matter.

It's a cliché that being a summer associate has nothing to do with being a lawyer and like many clichés, this has a ring of truth. While junior lawyers do get to wear a suit and do research assignments, there are some big differences to remember when you decide to start with a firm.

Summer associates get the best work. Because summer associates are temporary, they generally can't be put on long-running matters. Because summer associates have no useful skills other than legal research, they are often used on interesting research tasks to give them something to do. Because firms are trying to attract and retain summer associates, giving them menial/repetitive/boring but necessary work is looked down upon. Which law firm wants to gain the reputation of having forced all their summer associates to perform a 3 month discovery all summer?

A lot of law firm work is menial/repetitive/boring but necessary work. The more junior you are, the more likely you're going to be saddled with it. This work is often done at difficult hours, under pressure but without supervision. In my first 3 years at BigLaw I did the following:

- Spent two days reading an important document aloud to another lawyer for the purpose of catching errors.
- Worked from 6pm to 2am for multiple nights importing handwritten changes made by a senior lawyer to a 200 page document, and then checking each cross-reference individually.
- Worked multiple nights compiling lists of changes the other side had made to finance documents, and presenting them to my partner for his/her review.
- Spent 2 weeks reviewing the validity of a client's global trade mark portfolio as part of due diligence.
- Spent multiple weeks on the same discovery exercise, doing nothing but reviewing emails on a computer screen 12 hours a day.

I didn't have a bad experience at my firm (indeed most of my colleagues had worse jobs) but this is an example of the menial/repetitive/boring work you do as a lawyer that you don't do as a summer associate.

Summer associates have no pressure to meet billable targets; they are the protected species of law firms. Junior lawyers have real pressure to make their billable targets. The pressure on junior lawyers depends on the type of firm: if the firm allocates you to one partner, then that partner is obliged to provide you with work and if you don't get any work, it may not be your fault (though this doesn't mean you won't be blamed for this come performance review). However if you are in a more free-market atmosphere, where finding billable work from partners is part of your job, then the pressure to find billable work can be intense, especially if you are at a firm that is generally quiet.

Summer associates get to leave the matters that they worked on over summer behind at the end of the summer. As a junior lawyer, unless you are rotating out, you have your matters and you have to see them through. This means that you have to deal with the consequences of your earlier mistakes and short-cuts.

In short don't be misled by the summer associate life. You should use that time to evaluate the different practice groups that lawyers work in and how busy and satisfied they are. Work out how junior lawyers do their job and whether you want to follow in their footsteps. You know you don't have to be a BigLaw lawyer!

Lesson 3 – You are useless, and will only become less useless from practice

I used to describe junior lawyers as being like dogs (bear with me for this comparison). When they arrive at a law firm, they are like puppies: adorable and enthusiastic, but really only capable of crapping everywhere and ripping up things. As they get more experienced, they start to cause fewer hassles and start learning a few tricks (1 year lawyers), but, it takes a good two years for a junior lawyer to be able to look after him or herself and be properly trained.

Unless you have some previous experience you come to a law firm with good research and writing skills, and perhaps some legal knowledge, but have never run a matter, corresponded with an opposing lawyer, taken instructions from a client, drafted documents, negotiated with a real opponent or analyzed a document prepared by the other side for holes and gaps that could disadvantage your client (as an aside, would it kill law schools to offer a class on how to critically analyze a contract and redraft it to protect your client's interests!) You probably have no idea of what is 'market' in credit contracts, M&A transactions or property transactions. You may have no idea what a term sheet is, or how to prepare an originating process to commence a lawsuit.

Phew, that is a long list of things you're pretty useless at. Luckily, in BigLaw they don't expect you to be good at it the first day, and generally there are a few checks and balances in place to keep you from committing malpractice in your first few years. However, if you want to be a real lawyer you need to know some or all of the above and it's worthwhile learning it quickly. In the meantime law firms always have plenty of menial/repetitive/boring work to roll downhill to junior lawyers to keep them occupied while they learn the ropes.

Lesson 4 – All firms are the same except…

It is amazing that firms spend so much time promoting a 'distinctive workplace culture', a 'collaborative environment', and talk about their 'great range of clients'. Stop now: All BigLaw firms are the same.

While there are always exceptions, in summary, the top 5 firms/offices in your city are usually working for the same, or similar corporate clients, often on the same litigations or deals (opposed to each other). They all operate on the same business model, buying lawyer time in bulk and selling it to the client on a piece by piece basis, and then sharing the profits among the partners. They all have managing partners who are assisted by a variety of non-legal advisers (finance, HR, IT, external boards etc.) They all work in shiny offices with fit outs that are more or less the same, which are pretty cushy compared to the average office worker. They all pay at similar or identical rates, and they all have similar partnership promotion opportunities. They will all work junior lawyers exceptionally hard but tell you in the interview that they don't have a facetime culture (they probably don't, but just want you to work 12 hours a day). They all have similar social functions and offer secondments to similar clients.

In short, if you are agonizing over Skadden or Davis Polk, or A&O and Linklaters, or KWM and HSF, don't. From the perspective of a junior lawyer, the differences between the top tier firms are illusory. Even the differences between a top-tier and second-tier firm (for example Magic Circle and Silver Circle) are essentially illusory, so

- there is no need to be a prestige obsessive and go for the top firm if the second-tier firm is a better fit; and
- there is no point going to the second-tier firm because they won't work you as hard (short answer: They will).

There are a couple of possible exceptions to the rule that are worthwhile discussing.

Small or boutique specialist firms

The 'all firms are the same' rule does not apply to small firms. Small firms can be affected by one or two key partners' idiosyncrasies enormously, for good, or for evil. Boutique specialist firms, such as ones that only do IP litigation, or ones that only do white-collar criminal work, are a strange breed. In essence they have the same trappings as BigLaw firms (they work on the same business model), but because they only do certain types of work, they are measurably different than large corporate firms. For example, if you work for a patent litigation firm you'll never do any due diligence. If you work for a tax advisory firm, you'll probably be under less time pressure in your work than you would if you were doing transactions. Sometimes, because all the lawyers in the firm have a similar interest (tax, for example), there can be a shared intellectual culture in the way that a BigLaw firm simply doesn't have (Litigators think M&A lawyers aren't real lawyers, M&A lawyers think everyone else isn't pulling their weight, tax lawyers complain that everybody ignores them until the last minute etc.). Boutique specialist firms are worthwhile investigating, with the caveat that they often do not recruit graduates, and before you go in you better be certain that you want to stay in that area of law for the rest of your career as it is harder to move areas once you are in a small firm (because you can't move areas within a specialist firm and that firm will not have a reputation in the area of law you want to move to). The legal world is full of people who wanted to do x work, hated it and found satisfaction in y!

Particularly poorly run firms

In recent years, a number of US Law firms have dissolved as a result of the Great Rescission and potentially poor management decisions. Particularly poorly run law firms are a world of their own, and you should steer clear of them, unless you are particularly confident of your or its prospects.

There is a difference between poorly run firms and well-run firms that have been hit by a scandal. If there are 100 partners in an office, the fact that one of them has been caught misleading the court, or is being sued for professional misconduct, or has made a racist statement on social media will not affect the survival of a firm, or how well-run it is. Equally, don't ignore a firm because 10 partners have recently defected. Sometimes this means something; sometimes it doesn't. Do your research before you make the call.

Head office or branch offices

When in doubt, always try and work in the firm headquarters, or a large office of a firm. Small branch offices are vulnerable to the idiosyncrasies of the local managing partner, and can always be closed down by head office if they aren't paying their way. They may be dependent on a single client and if the client leaves, the branch office will be closed. Even larger branch offices are less than ideal. Morale can be slightly lower because 'head office never pays any attention to us'. Problems do get fixed quicker if the firm managing partner walks past them. Upgrades in technology and systems always happen in head office first, and the more senior you get, the more travel you will be stuck doing to the head office. In particular there are two very good reasons why you should try and work in a head office

- Issues with partner profitability in regional branch offices:

I summered with a branch office of a BigLaw law firm in a smallish city. The firm had particular PPP requirements that were the same for all offices. Unfortunately, the market in this city simply could not support the same billing rates that were charged at the firm headquarters. Therefore, either the partners priced themselves out of the market, or engaged in an absurd degree of leverage to hit their targets. Instead of 2-4 lawyers per partner, there were 4-8. Lawyers weren't paid what lawyers in headquarters were paid, and it was regarded as essentially impossible to be made a partner. For this reason, the branch office had major retention issues for its junior lawyers.

This may not be the case in all branch offices, but law firms often have a one-size fits all model that simply is not appropriate in many branch offices, and can make the practice of law less rewarding.

- Lunchtime CLEs

This is one of things that appears minor, but actually makes a significant impact on your life as a junior lawyer. As a junior lawyer you will be encouraged/required to go to lunchtime CLEs (Continuing Legal Education) where you will listen to a partner describe their greatest recent success as you munch on sandwiches, pizza, or the like. It is tolerable at head offices. However if you are at a branch office in a different time-zone, stuck in a little conference room with your colleagues, watching a video-conference screen for an hour (and it isn't even lunch), it is an annoying waste of time. There are usually a million other things you could be doing, but instead you are stuck in a dull little room for an hour. It's no fun and something that headquarters lawyers don't deal with.

Firms with a particular strategy for rewarding staff

These are rare, but certain firms have business strategy that includes paying staff considerably above the market rate, either in salary or bonuses. They are rare, and in many markets don't exist. They are often ambitious mid-tier firms seeking to attract staff, or boutique firms with a particularly solid client base, or even a top of the market firm that wishes to stay that way. These firms are measurably different to other law firms.

If you happen to discover such a law firm, investigate it closely to discover if there is a catch. Are they otherwise poorly-resourced? Is the strategy a temporary one? Are the bonus targets unreasonable? However, if you do find a firm that consistently pays above market rates and there is no obvious catch, then take the job. The differences between such a firm and a more 'established' firm that pays at, or below market are unlikely to make up for the higher salary. At either firm you will be in an office, working long hours for a partner. There will be technology problems, and the firm will nickel and dime you for savings. You may love or hate your partner at either firm and you'll work on similar matters. If you get offered the higher-paying job, you've done your research, and there is no obvious reason to reject the offer, don't overthink it—take the job.

Local vs National vs Global firms

One distinction that many junior lawyers think makes a difference, but really doesn't, is whether the firm is local, national or global, with the assumption that the global firm has better clients, offers better work and offers more interesting and international work. I am not talking about the difference between Baker & McKenzie and a suburban law firm, but between a top local corporate law firm in your city, a similarly resourced office that happens to be part of a broader national firm, and a similarly resourced office that happens to be part of a huge international firm. As a junior lawyer, your experience will be similar regardless of which firm you pick.

You will be working long hours in a nice office with partners who may be nice, or may be horrible. This is the essential element of law firm life, and does not vary according to the law firm. However let's have a look at the so-called advantages of the larger firms:

- Ooh we have an office in London, I've always wanted to work there!

Working in London is great: Go for it! However unless you are particularly lucky, no firm is simply going to transfer you to their London office based on your dream. They hired you to work in a particular office, for a particular set of partners. If you are good, they want to keep you there. There is generally no particular benefit for them to allow talented junior lawyers to move office. While some firms do allow a degree of movement within offices that is often either window-dressing (summer associate programs), or a recognition of the obvious (i.e. we were going to lose this lawyer otherwise, so let's make sure they move to the London office within our firm).

More importantly, if you want to work in London, do you necessarily want to work in your firm's London office? It may be a small satellite office, it may not offer the best pay and conditions, or it simply may not be the best fit for you. If you really want to work in London, then you should do what any other lawyer would do. Examine the market, find the firm that is the best fit, and move to that firm. Just because you worked in a 'global' firm, you are no better off than the lawyer who has spent a few years at the well-regarded local firm.

- We get to work on big national/international deals. I could travel to London to be part of a transaction!

A common misconception is that national/international firms do the big international deals while local firms act for local clients. While this depends on the size of the city and client base, that is generally untrue. Partners based in a city, regardless of what type of corporate law firm they are in, generally operate for clients in that city. If the clients are doing a big international deal they will work with their trusted partner, regardless of the structure of the law firm.

The mere fact that a firm happens to have an office in Bulgaria doesn't mean that they get a huge number of deals in Bulgaria. BigLaw clients are fairly sophisticated and have no problems engaging a top local law firm if it happens to suit their needs, especially if the alternative is a three person satellite office sent out by an ambitious managing partner in London/New York who wants to take over the world.

Furthermore, partners in national or multinational firms do plenty of local work. They have local clients who need contracts drafted, financing done, or litigation run locally. Again, clients will go with their trusted lawyer, regardless of the type of law firm he or she is part of.

In summary: When comparing otherwise similar law offices, in terms of reputation, size and work produced, do not assume the firm with an international network offers significantly better or more 'international' work.

Secondly, even if the international firm does offer more 'international work', any experienced lawyer would tell you that 'international work sucks!'. Lawyers talk about three-way conference calls between London, New York and Hong Kong: the reality of this is that someone is taking the call at 3.30 in the morning, if they are lucky from home, if not stuck in the office. International work also means getting a document at 9pm at night, with a request to get it back in 4 hours' time. It can mean endless miscommunications with clients who don't understand how things are done in your jurisdiction, and frustration with how the opposing counsel do things. Finally once you do the big sexy international deal that has destroyed your sleep habits and life for the past month, the clients aren't even around to take part in a celebratory lunch! Generally, deals with other local law firms run much smoother; there is a shared understanding of the procedure that needs to be followed, and there is a general appreciation of what terms are market and what terms are not.

Finally, a dirty little secret of corporate life is that business travel sucks. You should avoid it whenever possible. Watch 'Up in the Air'. You have a good, consistent life in your law firm. You commute in at (6-10am) and leave at (6pm-2am). You have weekends (sometimes) with your family and friends. Suddenly you are asked to go on a trip and find out that your commute got a lot longer and more painful. You are suddenly getting up at 3am to make the 6am flight. You are stuck on a plane for a few hours, without e-mail or internet access (most of the time), and arrive at your destination to find out all your other matters have gone crazy without you there. You are then stuck in an office, much like yours for 12 hours a day, potentially for days on end, and at the end of the day you either:

- go back to your hotel room, away from your friends and family;
- go out drinking with the locals to 'build relationships'. This leaves you jet-lagged and wrecked for the next week; or
- fly home, and arrive at home at some ungodly hour with piles more work to be done. Oh and they expect you back at the office at your normal time tomorrow.

Even if you are in an exotic location, you will spend your days in an office and conference room, and are unlikely to see anything more exciting than the local bar. I had a friend working in a Magic Circle firm who was put on a big deal in Moscow. For three months, she woke up at 3am on Monday morning for the first flight from Heathrow to Sheremetyevo, worked 15 hour days before collapsing in her hotel room, and flew back every Friday evening. She never saw any real part of Moscow, never had any particular engagement with the locals outside her firm, and gained no new experiences. She missed out on spending time with her husband and all the activities they could have done together on weeknights in London. That's what business travel is like in the legal world.

Lesson 5 – ...but partners vary enormously

If I could pass a simple lesson to every junior lawyer, it would be this: don't work for a bad partner. Nothing, not firm quality, work quality, support, location, pay or work-load, affects the life of a junior lawyer more than the quality of a partner. A good partner can make the practice of law an engaging, challenging, and even fun experience. A bad partner can make the practice of law pure hell. The worst of it is that some inexperienced lawyers stuck with a bad partner think 'well this is what it is like in a big firm' and trundle on, not realizing that they are stuck in an abusive workplace relationship.

When I'm talking about a good or bad partner, I'm not talking about social skills or quality of work, but rather what they are like to work for. There are no shortage of partners who are engaging, successful, even inspirational but make their staff's lives a living hell. At the same time, there are partners who are socially awkward, a little bit unfriendly, and even shout a bit, but can be great to work for.

There are all sorts of bad partners. There is the partner who is charming, engaging, and enthusiastic, but with no managerial skills. This partner loads staff up with non-billable work, and then screams at them if they didn't meet their billable targets. They don't allow their team to leave before they do. They force their team to attend hour long motivational talks. They leak staff constantly, and are constantly recruiting and training new staff and begging every remaining staff member to stay. For those of you who think I am exaggerating, there is a partner like this in every BigLaw office in the world.

There is the well-regarded, affable partner with a great client base, who decides you aren't cut out to be part of their team, and starves you of work. They may not be a bad partner but they are a bad partner for you

There's the funny, social, very well-regarded partner who is excellent with clients. However, this partner is so busy with clients, that they are completely disorganized in running their team. Documents that needed to be reviewed wait in their in-tray for weeks, forcing team members to lie to clients and other lawyers. This partner then suddenly realizes, on a Friday afternoon, that a task had to be done on Monday morning and drops it on their lawyers at 6pm on a Friday, even though it has been in their in-tray for a week. E-mails go unanswered, and documents are sent out unreviewed.

A good partner is pleasant to staff and does not pass the pressure down. Documents are promptly and consistently reviewed. They take an interest in the development of staff. Because they are efficient in their practice, they and their team are often able to leave at a reasonable hour. They are able to keep a loyal, well-oiled team around them who know their roles and like each other.

There are any number of ways a partner can be a good or a bad partner but the simplest test is: Does s/he make your job easier or harder. Below is a table summarizing the sort of behaviors that good and bad partners engage in. Note that no one partner is perfect 100% of the time and no one partner is terrible 100% of the time, rather these are common behaviors that good and bad partners demonstrate.

A Good Partner...	A Bad Partner...	With these consequences:
Generally gives you prompt instructions with enough time to do the task.	Sits on work, and gives it out when convenient to them which can lead to	You waste nights and weekends unnecessarily with a bad partner.

	impossible deadlines.	
Gives you clear instructions, makes sure you write them down and responds to any questions you have. S/he also explains the deadline for the project and how much time s/he expects you to spend on it. S/he may also explain the broader purpose of their instructions but this isn't necessary.	Gives you hurried instructions while doing something else, and gets annoyed if you try and clarify your task.	You don't waste time with a good partner. A bad partner may not even be sure what they want, as evidenced by their hurried instructions. You are likely to 'get it wrong'. Also a partner who doesn't set a deadline doesn't enable you to prioritize your work, making you less efficient.
Is available (either in person, phone or by e-mail) to respond to any questions you have once you have done some initial work. I.e. Did you want me to investigate xyz? S/he then gives clear answers.	Is unavailable or too busy to assist.	You don't spend more time on the project and you are more likely to get it right.
Reviews your work in advance of any particular deadline (i.e. if you need to get it back to the client by COB Friday, s/he has it reviewed by Friday	Doesn't review your work on time.	A bad partner makes you look bad to the client and other side.

lunch.		
Is reasonably clear in reviewing your work and, if necessary, provides feedback (sometimes feedback is obvious in the comments).	Is unclear in his edits (large crosses, 'Change this', 'wrong!', unclear handwriting) and never provides feedback or explanation for his changes.	Again if you can understand what the boss wants, you can do a better job of providing it.
Is fair when a mistake has been made, and looks at what needs to be done to prevent that mistake happening in the future.	Gets angry at you for 'your mistake' regardless of how the mistake occurred.	When a mistake is made you feel terrible. Being yelled at never helps.

Notice that in summarizing the good and bad qualities of partners, I haven't talked about how personable they are, their demeanor, their mentoring skills, or their legal abilities. As a junior lawyer, you depend on a partner's organization and communication skills. A well-organized partner who can communicate what s/he wants you to do can make work a pleasure. If you have a disorganized, haphazard partner who doesn't know what they want, or can't or won't communicate what they want, be prepared to waste a lot of time, lose a lot of nights and weekends and suffer unwarranted and unnecessary stress.

The behaviors above are really important in ensuring that you can do the job to the best of your abilities. The behaviors below relate to general demeanor and approach to work.

A Good Partner...	A Bad Partner...	With these consequences
Is at least vaguely affable in interactions.	Is always grumpy, angry or unpleasant.	You don't need to work for a saint, just a half decent human being.
Absorbs pressure from above (clients, management) and does not pass it down.	Passes pressure along down 'if we don't get this right for the client we'll lose them' or 'the client is really angry with your work on this matter'.	A junior lawyer isn't responsible for client relationships or for the work presented to the client. A good partner takes responsibility for his/her team, whatever they do.
Treats all staff members in his/her team fairly.	Plays favorites.	A partner may have a trusted team member but it is his/her job to work with and help develop all the members of the team.
Is generally available to discuss professional development, feedback and other concerns.	Is unavailable and doesn't listen.	Partners are busy people and not saints, but a good partner should be available for at least brief chats to junior lawyers.
Generally will have at least one senior lawyer working for them who has worked with the partner for a long time and knows what is going on.	Has no lawyers who are more than 3 years out of law school.	A senior lawyer is a lifesaver to work for. They can check your work before you take it to the partner, they can explain what a matter is all about, and you can ask

		them stupid questions. The presence of a senior lawyer makes your work so much easier. The absence of a senior lawyer suggests that the partner can't hold on to staff.
Knows the law and understands what is going on in his/her matters.	Doesn't understand the law or the details of the matters being worked on.	Surprisingly, it is not vital for partners to be great technical lawyers (a good senior lawyer/senior associate can be a lifesaver in this situation), but a partner who doesn't understand the law or the matter that they are working on cannot adequately supervise a junior lawyer. It is unfairly stressful to be asked to make calls as a 2nd year lawyer because the partner does not understand, or alternatively have to pass on incorrect advice because the partner does not know the matter or the law well-enough.

Is professional.	Is unprofessional.	While partners are human and occasionally get angry, drunk, cheat on their partners or say stupid things, you shouldn't work in an environment where a partner is abusive, sexist, racist, homophobic or has a substance abuse problem. If you are spending your time covering for or picking up the pieces for an unprofessional partner, leave. It will never end up well for your career or your sanity.

Your aim, as a junior lawyer, should not be to work in the greatest law firm in the world, or the sexiest practice area, but it should be to work with a good partner. Nothing will affect your life as a junior lawyer more than whether you work for a good partner or a bad partner. It can literally be the difference between having a good life and being a tear-stained workaholic.

The big question is how you end up with a good partner. It's not easy to do so, especially in the early years where you are simply assigned a partner/group. Another issue is that good partners retain staff easily and rarely have vacancies while bad partners constantly churn through staff. However you have put yourself in a good position by simply knowing the importance of a good partner. So what do you do?

How to identify the good partner/the bad partner to work for

This is harder than it looks since appearances can be deceiving. Some of the most successful, engaging and well-regarded partners in the firm can be bad partners to work for (although some of them may be successful because they are good to work for). Good partners can be gruff, awkward, and potentially a bit scary. Many bad partners succeed in hiding their disorganization through the heroic efforts of their team. Don't be deceived by good impressions or by who is a 'star', look deeper.

Talk to people, especially people who work for those partners, or used to work for those partners. Everybody gossips about partners. Filter out the 50% of gossip and rumor, but the remainder will have some spectrum of truth. Is the partner commonly described as 'the worst partner to work with at the firm'? Has the partner ever thrown a folder at a junior lawyer (an embarrassingly common occurrence in the law)? Is the partner known for giving out work on Friday afternoon due on Monday (a sure sign of a disorganized and inconsiderate partner)? Does the partner like to have long team meetings to motivate the team (not a disqualifying factor, but really good partners don't waste their staff's time with meetings)? Many lawyers have a degree of Stockholm syndrome with their bad partners, e.g.

> 'Yes I work long hours and get screamed at often but s/he always takes me out to lunch when the deal is over'

so ask them about their partner's work style. How do they give work? How do they give feedback? How do they go in retaining staff? Do they have any staff who have been with them for more than three years? Also consider whether a partner has a work style that fits your style. Are they otherwise a great partner, but expect their staff to get in at 7am because they likes to assign work then?

Are they good to work for if you are a man, but treat junior female lawyers poorly (a sadly too-common occurrence in law firm partners, whether male or female)?

Through this process, you may not necessarily identify who is the perfect partner for you to work for, but you should be able to identify who not to work for. It is easier to leave an average partner (who can replace you) than a bad partner (who is constantly scrabbling for staff and trying to keep all the staff they have).

How to get the good partner

This is the hard part. Junior lawyers don't always control where they go, and sometimes they are simply allocated by HR into teams that need them. However there are a couple of useful strategies you can try:

- Ask the Partner

I had a friend who was with a difficult partner and identified a better partner. S/he walked into his office one day and said 'I currently work with X, however I know you have an excellent practice that works well with my interest in y. I'd like to be considered the next time you have a vacancy in your team'. Three months later s/he was in his team.

- Do work for the Partner

Again, easier said than done, but there is nothing stopping you from offering to assist in their matters and contributing in some way to their team. This is particularly possible if you are in the same team or geographically close to them.

- Have a good record generally

Good partners have their pick of the junior lawyers. They aren't going to pick the average junior lawyer. Be good at what you do.

- Try and move into their team or geographically nearby

Again you may not get your dream partner, but at least if you are working in the same team you may work with them, and impress them, or at least chat them up at team drinks. However don't deliberately work for a bad partner just to be in the same team as the good partner. The good partner may not want to damage their relationship with the bad partner by stealing their staff.

- Keep trying

A lot of law firms have rotation programs which allow junior lawyers to work in two or three different groups. Sometimes you may be unfortunate enough to be stuck with bad partners in all your rotations. Try and move again, or get an additional rotation. It may look bad in the short term but it is better than being stuck with a bad partner. If you are stuck with a bad partner, consider moving firms. It may be no panacea but it beats spending your life with a bad boss. Remember all firms are the same, but partners vary enormously.

Lesson 6 – Practice groups matter more than firms but less than partners

This is not an easy section to write, because practice groupings vary enormously between firms. Some firms split practice groups by client groupings (Energy and Resources, Technology, Banking, etc.), while other firms by the type of work done (Tax advisory, M&A, Insurance litigation). The sort of work done by firms varies by country as do the legal stereotypes. In particular the presence of specialist barristers makes practicing as a litigator in the UK and Australia a very different experience to practicing litigation in the US and Canada.

For the purpose of this section I have divided up the work done by BigLaw firms into three broad categories – Deals, Litigation and Advisory. These categories can be sliced and diced in many ways, and in particular, advisory work is done both by specialist advisory groups (Tax advisory) and throughout the firm (litigators advising on prospects of success, M&A lawyers advising on structuring a deal). However it is reasonable to suggest that whether you work for a litigation, deals or advisory partner will strongly influence what work you do and determine how your career progresses.

One more piece of advice: If you are interested in progressing in a firm, pick the most boring-sounding practice area and target it. Everyone wants to be an IP litigator or work in constitutional law, but there is only so much work that is going around. The areas that are boring sounding always have good clients (otherwise there would be no practice), and because of the unglamorous nature of the work, often have retention issues, improving your prospects of getting in the group, staying in, and progressing to partner. An oft-told anecdote at my old firm is about a summer associate in 2000, who, in his interview, said he was very interested in the (then unglamorous and not at all notorious) world of securitization, and spoke persuasively about it in his interview. Apparently the securitization partners were so delighted that they had finally found someone genuinely interested in securitization that they begged the summer associate hiring committee to employ him, made sure he ended up in their team and (helped by his own talent and hard work), he is now a securitization partner.

Deals

This category includes M&A work, most banking work, and work in various practice areas described as 'front-end'. While this varies from firm to firm, and partner to partner, in some ways doing deals is the hardest and most punishing area of BigLaw to work in, especially on large M&A deals. A junior M&A lawyer can expect late nights, lots of conference calls, frantic last minute changes, and the exhaustion and elation that follows a signing (and they do the best celebrations afterwards).

Deals work is hard and punishing work because clients are hard and punishing. A deal normally has to be completed to a particular deadline, and the terms of the deal and supporting documentation may need to be redrafted at short notice. If you are working on a single deal, it is not uncommon to have nothing to do all day (and hence no billables) until 5pm when the other side sends you the documents, with a polite request that you get them back to them the next morning. This will suddenly send the team into a flurry of exhausted action. The time pressure is magnified if you have international clients who insist on conducting a conference call at 11pm at night, and then ask for documents to be ready in the few hours following the conference call. Tempers can be short, and burn-out is common.

On the bright side, doing deals is often the fastest way to partnership. Working on a deal is incredibly lucrative for firms, and if you are good at it, clients will recognize your skills. My opinion is that great M&A lawyers (by that, I mean a lawyer who is a superb negotiator, detail-oriented, knows how to conceptualize a matter and express it in a document, and can operate for days on no sleep), are born, not made, and the great ones go straight to the top. Furthermore a good deals team can develop a tremendous esprit de corps. The late nights, the teamwork, the long lunches afterwards can build a friendship and sprit that is often absent in other practice groups. Finally, a junior lawyer who is good at deals can work anywhere in the common law world. Want to move to a top commercial law firm in New York? Your UK tax advisory skills are of limited use, as is your understanding of Canadian civil procedure, however if you know how to draft a document and negotiate it under time pressure and little sleep, there will always be a job for you in the Big Apple. Equally, making the transition from working in deals to a less pressured legal counsel role is also easy.

As a personal note, I would never recommend working in deals unless you truly love it. The nature of the work is such that it becomes an all-consuming obsession. If you are not a natural, it can affect your health, your sanity, and your relationship or ability to form one. There is a world outside commercial deals that is much more interesting than junior lawyers in BigLaw think. However, if you want that lifestyle and the potential for significant rewards, go into it with open eyes.

Litigation

Litigation is what you probably imagined doing when you started at law school. All that running down to court, objecting to evidence and informing witnesses that they could not handle the truth! In the real world, litigation can be very different.

As noted above, the presence of barristers in the UK and Australia makes practicing commercial litigation in a BigLaw firm very different to practicing in Canada and the US. In Canada and the US, if you work in a large litigation group, your partners will generally be arguing significant matters in court, and, as more junior lawyers, you will have the opportunity to appear in depositions or smaller motions. In the UK and Australia, courtroom roles are generally (though not always) taken by barristers, and you will be spending much more time preparing evidence, doing legal research and negotiating settlements. This means that if you desperately want to have a practice focused on courtroom appearance work, you should strongly consider joining the Bar.

Litigation is generally a less stressful area of the law to practice in than deals, and one in which a good partner can make a significant difference. This is because, in the broadest sense, clients are generally unreasonable and courts are generally reasonable. In M&A, your client might ask you to negotiate and finalize a transaction involving thousands of pages of documents in three weeks, and then announce the terms have changed with a week to go. In litigation, a court might give you three months to prepare your evidence, which might be 5 affidavits with a total page count of 2000 pages (including exhibits). Even then, if you miss a deadline in litigation, it may be possible to get an extension from the court or your opponent. In M&A, a client might not be so accepting. While the pressure and workload in litigation increases during a trial, when a deadline is near, or if the team is understaffed generally, it is generally less pressured than deals. Equally, in litigation you are generally unlikely to have the situation, so common in deals, where you do no billable work all day but you have to work all night, and end up spending 16 hours at work for 9 billable hours. Generally, unless the practice is quiet, if you are at work you should be able to do billable work, be it research, drafting letters, or preparing evidence. The hours may still be long, and consistently long, but you will have fewer manic 24 hour stretches than in deals.

The difference between countries with, and without barristers becomes pronounced during a trial. In countries without barristers, the partner or lead litigator has to appear in court and hence has to get on top of cross-examination, evidentiary objections and legal arguments. It can be extraordinarily stressful to do that while still managing a practice and reviewing the work team members. Equally, if you are allergic to appearing in court, then you may not want to develop your career in the litigation field in these countries.

Countries with an independent bar operate quite differently. The barrister has to absorb the material and, often with the assistance of the instructing solicitor, prepares the legal arguments. The barrister prepares the cross-examination, oral submissions and evidentiary objections and incurs the stress of the appearance. Paradoxically, this means that during a hearing, a junior lawyer often has little to do other than watch the barrister, hand up appropriate documents and make appropriate notes. There may be days where the junior lawyer is asked to assist in preparing new evidence, or doing legal research in the evenings, but quite often during court proceedings, a junior lawyer doesn't actually have to do much.

This means that in countries without an independent bar, working in litigation is a higher-pressure endeavor with consequently higher rewards. In countries with an independent bar, BigLaw litigation can be a highly enjoyable area to practice because the work is consistent, at times interesting, and unless you have a bad partner, generally has less deadline pressure than deals.

Advisory

This is a hard area of the law to generalize because advisory work is an essential part of a junior lawyer's practice. It is also an area that is most often slotted in industry-based teams (IT might advise on patent law) or broader teams (IP litigation might also advise on prospects of a case or on whether a new business might infringe a competitor's IP), however there are practice areas (most commonly in tax) and partners that specialize in advisory work.

In short, if you like the work, advisory is a great area to work in. Unless you are needed to give advice on a deal at the last minute (and this will happen), the hours are good, the deadlines are often pretty reasonable, the workflow is often consistent, and there can be a great intellectual challenge in the work.

So, what's the downside? Firstly many lawyers find the work grinding and boring. You're only a young lawyer once. Don't you want to be going to court or working on a billion dollar deal instead of looking at footnotes in cases that may assist in the interpretation of a sub-clause of the Tax Act? Do you really want to have 24 different tabs open on your computer as you try and track the use of a definition through a complex piece of litigation? Do you want to review the law in 50 different states (US) or the EU (UK lawyers) as it applies to your issue? The work is hard and grinding, and if it doesn't suit your personality, can be soul-destroying. Secondly, if you like working as a team, advisory isn't the place for you. Your work will be doing research and drafting by yourself, subject to the occasional interrogation by your partner about having ignored some long forgotten case. You won't spend as much time working as a team, considering broad strategy with reference to an upcoming case, or an upcoming deal, although if you are advising on a new product (such as in financial services advisory) you may have the satisfaction of designing or re-designing a product to reduce legal risk.

Also, unless you are in a very specialist field, such as tax advisory, partnership prospects are not always the strongest. The reason is that all lawyers think that they can do advice work, so why would they necessarily come to you to advise them on (for example), legislation governing the regulation of corporations, when they could get a specialist corporations litigator, who also knows the law, and their team to advise at the same time. As such, in order to build a practice it is often worthwhile developing a specialist expertise, either in law or in an industry that is not replicated elsewhere in the firm, so you can be, for example, the specialist in anti-money laundering, or the one who knows all about the law governing offshore oil exploration. Alternatively, you could try and keep your hand in and develop your skills as a litigator or deal-maker so you can assist in their matters while preserving your expertise in your advisory areas.

Chapter 2 - How not to get fired (and they will fire you)

Now, it comes to the most important part of the book. Every year junior lawyers are 'performance managed' out of law firms, gently suggested that they might find other careers, or even outright fired. Sometimes, it is a relief for the junior lawyer, as they were a bad fit anyway, but for most junior lawyers, some of whom have families to support, debts to pay and limited prospects of getting as well-paying a job, it can be devastating.

Different firms have different policies on firing staff, and of course they all 'want you to succeed and provide you with training and mentorship to help you be the best lawyer you can be'. But, realistically, they all have cut-offs (to prove that you are competent) before you start being 'performance-managed'. Sometimes, it is two years in when the firm decides whether you are of value to the firm, or you don't and never will 'get it' and aren't going to contribute to the firm going forward. Indeed in the UK, most graduate solicitors sign 2 year training contracts, after which the firm will decide whether they are worth keeping on further.

This chapter is about how to make it to the two-four year period with a reputation as a good, decent lawyer within your firm. It is not about how to make partner, as that is something well-down the track and is significantly affected by things that are outside your control (the market, the performance of your firm, whether your firm has just lost a client, whether you have a powerful partner in your corner). Rather, it focuses on the key things you can do early in your firm to ensure that you can make a success of your time as a junior lawyer and either push on to become a person on a partner track, or leave on your own terms to follow your dream.

While there are many mistakes a junior lawyer can make, there are two key ones that lead to 90% of the firings/performance management issues for junior lawyers. They are being a dick and not doing the work. These may be obvious but you'd be amazed at how often junior lawyers make these mistakes.

Lesson 1 - Don't be a dick

You are working as part of a team. You are working long hours together. You are the least important person in that team (and that includes the legal secretary, WP operator and person who makes the partner's coffee [to a partner, a junior lawyer is replaceable, while a good barista is worth their weight in gold]). Why the hell would a partner want their team to include a person who is difficult to work with?

Side note: your partner may be 'difficult'. They may yell at their secretary, they may be grumpy, they may swear, and they may make idiotic statements. They are, within limits, allowed to do those things. They are an important person who the firm values enough to make a co-owner. The firm could replace you tomorrow and never notice the difference.

You should know how not to be a difficult, however, for those of you who need an explanation, here is an incomplete catalogue of things not to do as a junior lawyer.

Never be rude to a partner

This includes getting angry with them when they give you work, or even complaining or sighing loudly. There is no need for sarcasm either. You're an adult, it's their job to give you work. Be professional about this and never make a partner feel bad about giving you work. If they don't want to give you work, then you don't have a job.

Never be rude to anyone else, in particular never be rude to secretaries, cleaners or other support staff

I cannot stress this enough: be pleasant to everybody! This includes 10pm at night, 6am in the morning, or when somebody has stuffed up. This doesn't mean being a doormat if somebody is in the wrong, but never raise your voice, throw everything, or insult somebody.

Every year entitled young law graduates come to law firms thinking that because they have a law degree, they can boss around secretaries and other junior staff. If you are rude to a secretary, this will get passed along to the other secretaries (the secretary network is powerful) and either:

- none of the secretaries will work for you, or will do your work slowly and slovenly; and/or
- a partner will find out.

If you ever get into a situation where you cannot work with the legal secretary, remember that they have been around longer than you, have more connections within the firm, know where the partner buries their bodies, and are much harder to replace than you are. Equally, if you are ever abusive to a more junior lawyer or support staff, people will find out, and you'll get a reputation as either a bully, or someone who is utterly two-faced, sucking up to those who are more important than you and being abusive to those 'less important'. No partner is going to want to have one of those people in their team if they can help it, and you'll have the choice of either leaving the firm or being stuck with the bad partner who can't hold on to better junior lawyers.

Finally, if you are ever rude to someone more junior than you, at some point you will find that you'll desperately need that secretary/clerk/paralegal/summer associate to do something for you that is above and beyond the call of duty. They won't do it if they don't like you, and you'll be embarrassed. Don't take that risk.

Never make sexist, homophobic, racist or otherwise demeaning comments

Now this is a hard lesson to learn. Some people enjoy making ironically politically incorrect statements. Some people want to curry

favor with politically incorrect partners. Some people have just
broken out of a bad relationship and want to explain how 'all men
are pigs/all women are bitches'. Some people like to look at breasts.
As a junior lawyer, keep your mouth shut and your behavior
appropriate. A senior lawyer, with a sterling reputation, deep
connections within the firm, and an understanding of how the office
works and who might be offended by what, can get away with
making ironic comments. A partner, who is a valued member of the
firm, may even be able to get away with blatantly offensive
comments. As a junior lawyer, you haven't been around long
enough to know how your comment will be taken or who will take
offence. If a complaint is made about you, you don't have enough of
a reputation to justify keeping you/survive being known as the 'the
Homophobe' or 'the Racist'.

Never be 'too good' for the work

Law firms give junior lawyers menial/boring/repetitive work. That is
a fact of life and the reality of having a great degree but little or no
skills to survive the BigLaw experience. You may have an honors
degree from Cambridge with an expertise in international arbitration,
but your job now may be to go through thousands of pages of due
diligence documents, day after day, until you are told to stop. If you
take this job with a smile, work hard at it and do well, you'll get
better jobs. If you refuse it, avoid it, do the minimum necessary, or
do a sloppy job with it, the next time better work comes along you
won't be called upon, and there is no way a partner (who actually
knows how to practice law and deliver what his clients want), wants
to have in their team a person who thinks they are too good for the
work they have to do. Don't worry, practicing law does get more
interesting in a few years (more on this later), or you could go back to
academia or into policy, but once you are hired as a junior lawyer,
you are there to do their work, and do it well.

A further sin is lying about being too busy to do the
boring/menial/repetitive work. If your response to being asked to go

into a due diligence is 'I can't, I'm working on a big matter with x', there is every chance that X will find out. Equally if you just say that you're really busy, people will see your empty office at 7pm, or you checking Facebook at 9.30 the next morning. A bad reputation is contagious and having a reputation as an untrustworthy, malingering liar will guarantee your time at the firm will be short and unpleasant.

Never play office politics in your early years and only work with 'important' senior lawyers

Law firms are a hive of politics. Some are better at office politics than others but all firms have people who play the political game well. You might be inspired by the SA who always seems to get the best gigs and is on the fast track to partnership. They may be good at office politics. You are not. Don't play the game.

As a junior lawyer, your aim is to be well-regarded by everyone. You cannot afford to make an enemy or be seen to be the office crawler/gunner (and hated by everyone else). You don't know the contours of the office, you don't know the rules of the game, and you don't know the connections. That loser of a counsel/special counsel you just told a joke about to a partner—that counsel and partner may be old friends who started at the firm together. The person whose work you blew off because they weren't important may become important in the next few years, and probably has a long memory and good connections.

Particularly egregious are junior lawyers who refuse work from, or do poor work for some senior lawyers because they aren't 'important' enough, or don't work in the areas that they want to go to. Brushing off people (and lying about it) or only doing your best work for certain lawyers is a sure way to trash your reputation.

An example of this happened at my BigLaw firm: a summer associate refused work from a first year lawyer because s/he had a pro bono task to do. The junior lawyer was later asked by her partner whether she thought the associate should be part of the team going forward. You can guess what her answer was. While it is unlikely that the junior lawyer's opinion was definitive, a summer associate's decision to ignore a more senior lawyer's request for assistance for silly reasons helped cost him/her a position in the team as a graduate.

Never play office politics and try and compete with other junior lawyers

Sure, you could take the view that the other junior lawyers are competition; after all there are only so few partnership slots/jobs with the good partners around. It may be tempting to try and play office politics with them or try and beat them to get the good work, or just generally try and compete with the other lawyers. It is a foolhardy and short term strategy.

Here's why. BigLaw is a marathon not a sprint, and you'll get a lot further by being well-liked and respected by your colleagues than by getting that extra assignment in October of your 2nd year. You never know where you colleagues will end up. They might make partner ahead of you and be responsible for considering your application. They may end up legal counsel, choosing whether to engage you, or another lawyer. They may end up on the opposite side of the deal. They may end up being completely unimportant to your career but are friends with those who have an important role to play. You don't want them to think that you are two-faced and untrustworthy. Help your colleagues. Bond with them. Advise them, support them and do all you can for them. Not only will you feel good, but it will be good for your career.

Lesson 2 - Do the work, all the work

The most important thing you can do in your first years as a junior lawyer is to build trust with senior lawyers and partners. You have a wonderful pedigree and brilliant marks. So does everyone else. The way to stay and progress at a firm is for more senior lawyers to give you work so you bill your hours and develop your skills. However, this only happens if they trust you to do what they ask, when they ask it. The work may seem to be small and unimportant, but how you perform it may have an outsize impact on your reputation.

Look at it from the perspective of a senior lawyer. You are running a large commercial transaction. Documents have come in from the other side and you need to get them to the client in 12 hours for their review. You make a number of handwritten changes in a document and give it to a junior lawyer and say 'incorporate them in tracked changes. If I have changed a defined term in one place, change it in the rest of the document and update the table of contents and make sure all the automatic cross-referencing works. Give it to me in 10 hours so I can review it by then'. If you haven't received the document 10 hours later you:

- have to follow-up with the junior lawyer, which you shouldn't have to do.
- have to listen to their explanation as to why it wasn't done; and
- have to explain to the client why you haven't hit your deadline, which is professionally embarrassing for you; or
- have to drop everything and do the work yourself, which throws the rest of your job out of whack, and might result in you staying late.

In short you will be exceedingly angry with the junior lawyer, and not only will you never trust that lawyer with work again (the lawyer has stuffed up a simple task and embarrassed you), you will bitch about him/her to all your colleagues.

This is even worse when the recipient of the work is a partner. Imagine if a partner has a call with a client at 3pm and has asked you to provide them with a 2 page research memo by 2pm so they can review the law before advising the client. If they don't get the document in time they are going to be embarrassed with their client and furious with you. Even if they are pleasant and understanding with you (and some partners are), they are unlikely to give you a second chance.

In short, the easiest way to lose trust and damage your reputation is not to do the work. There may be a good reason (in your mind) for this. You may have other work that you prioritize first. A more senior partner has given you work that is urgent. You may have had a personal issue. You may have misunderstood the deadline. The work may have taken longer than expected. If you don't immediately inform the senior lawyer of these good reasons and instead leave it to the last minute and make them look bad, the senior lawyer may lack trust in you going forward.

If there is a problem, either solve it yourself, or let the senior lawyer know and let them know as soon as possible. If you have two equally urgent tasks, see if someone else can assist you with one of them (and tell the senior lawyer what is happening). If that isn't possible let the senior lawyer know and s/he'll tell you whether to prioritize his/her task, whether s/he can re-assign it or whether it is no longer that urgent. If you don't understand the deadline, check, and never as a junior lawyer make assumptions about how long something will take. If it's your first time, it will always take longer than expected. If you are going to miss the deadline, report it as soon as possible and see if you can bring a solution to the senior lawyer. The worst thing to do is simply not do the work by the deadline and hope it will be all right. You will get a reputation for being a bad junior lawyer and that is difficult to recover from.

For the same reason, don't overpromise and under-deliver. If you tell a senior lawyer you will have something to them in an hour, and don't give it to them for two hours they have potentially wasted an hour of their time waiting for you. They are not happy, and are unlikely to trust you.

Lesson 3 - Bill the work, all the work

Firm policy varies as to billing requirements but unless they tell you otherwise, bill every piece of time you spend on the matter. There are two stupid mistakes that junior lawyers make.

Failing to complete time-sheets promptly and accurately

Short of doing the work, there is nothing more important to a firm than putting in your timesheets (some firms would regard putting in your time as more important than doing the work). The tools are there. It's not hard and it will aggravate partners no end if you don't put in your time by the end of every day or the morning after at the very latest. The firm can't bill unless you put in your time. It also affects your performance and how you will be measured.

Entering your time late affects the bills sent to clients which can annoy them (clients don't like to be sent a surprisingly large bill for work done 2 months ago), and it affects your performance. One of the basic things about law firms is that if you get the little, simple things right (like putting in your time, doing the work and not being 'difficult') you can vastly improve your prospects of progressing. Get into good habits from day 1, and make sure that you have a mechanism for recording your time, and that you always have it entered at the end of the day.

Self-discounting their time

'Oh I'm an idiot. I spent three hours researching this question only to realize I was in the wrong jurisdiction. I can't possibly bill this to the client (I'd basically be committing fraud), and I can't let my partner see what an idiot I am, I better not record this time'.

Record that time! You may have gone down the wrong path and may feel bad about the client being billed for your wasted time. However that is not your decision to make. That is your partner's decision. They sign off on the bills, and they decide what can be written off. It may be that they were actually expecting you to spend six hours on the project, you wasted 3 and then got it done in 3. You don't know the situation, and it's not your call to make.

Also by writing off time you are affecting your own performance. You are measured by the time you bill, not only for performance and bonuses, but also how busy you are. Some partners, when they are allocating work, look at how their team is billing and simply give the new work to the lowest billing lawyer. Do you want to be unfairly loaded with work because the guy next to you puts all his time in, and you don't? Do you want the guy next to you to get a billable hours bonus and you not to because you don't put your time in?

Now there is one possible exception to the rule, and this is when you work at a firm which closely monitors billable yield (i.e. the amount of time not written off and billed to the client). Sometimes both lawyers and partners are evaluated by how little of their time (or their team's time) is written off. If you are under the gun for having too much time written off, that is a tough position to be in, since you can't control that. My advice there would be to keep billing all your time and have a discussion with the partner about how you can reduce the amount of time written off (i.e. how to be more efficient).

A more difficult situation is when your partner is under pressure to reduce their write-offs and hints ('You shouldn't take more than 1 hour on this letter' [when they know it will take 2]), implies ('You've been spending too long on these affidavits. Is there any way we can reduce the time') or asks ('Don't record your time for this task') you to self-discount your time. In my view, and in the view of much of the profession, this is inappropriate. You are measured by your billables, and you shouldn't have your performance reduced because your partner can't have an appropriate discussion with the client about fees. Equally the partner, by asking you not to record your time, is deceiving the firm. The firm sells billable targets and needs to know how many hours its lawyers are working and whether partners are working for clients that pay less than the firm wants.

However it does happen, and it is very difficult to say no to a partner. My approach would be:

- Send an e-mail to the partner when completing the work confirming that you have self-discounted. Get a paper trail.
- Check with the firm's internal staffing people (or even better, ask a friend to check anonymously) about what the firm's policy is on self-discounting, especially when it is requested by a partner. Some firms have very strong policies that this is unacceptable, while others are more lenient.
- If it is a one-off or an occasional request, let it go. It's not worth having a fight with your partner about it. If it is consistent, go to a senior partner in the team and talk to them about it. You could even frame it as a request for advice 'My partner is asking me to self-discount my time. What should I do?' If they are concerned about it they'll talk to your partner about it, and it may stop. If your partner gets angry at you either:
  - o Blame another person—say you were bitching about it, and somebody must have gone to the partner; or
  - o Look to move on – unless the partner is an otherwise wonderful human being, you don't want to work for somebody who victimizes their junior for reporting a breach of firm policy.

Lesson 4 - Don't waste people's time

Partners and senior lawyers are extraordinarily busy people. They often have a to-do list a mile long, and if they have a junior lawyer who consistently wastes their time then that junior lawyer will not get work from them. Your job is to take work off a partner's plate and not to put work back on. You put work back on their plate by:

- Not doing the work (see lesson 2)
- Doing the work poorly

- Constantly interrupting them, or asking for assistance for tasks that you could have done yourself had you exercised a moment of thought.

Good partners and senior lawyers know that a stich in time saves nine and, if you push them, they will spend the time and effort with you to avoid the issues above. You just need to take the right steps.

The lessons relating to not being 'difficult' and doing the work are the difference between a poor-to-average junior lawyer and a fired junior lawyer. The timesaving tips below and in the next few lessons are the difference between being an average junior lawyer and a good junior lawyer—one who senior lawyers will fight to have.

Timesaving Tip 1 – when receiving instructions take good notes.

Whenever I was asked to see a senior lawyer or partner, I always took a pad of paper. I almost got in the habit of carrying a pad of paper around just in case anything happened. If you are caught without a pad and pen, stop the instructions and ask to grab one. It will annoy the partner but not as much as not remembering the instructions. I've got terrible handwriting so when I got out of the partner's office, I used to go back to my office, and type out all the instructions so I had a clear picture of what I needed to do.

Timesaving Tip 2 – when receiving instructions, ask the right questions

When is this due by? How do you want it (e-mail, letter, memo, in-person chat)? How much time should I be spending on it (if it is a research task and it is unclear, ask what the scope is?). Then at the end of the instruction repeat back to your partner exactly what it is that you will be doing. You may look like an idiot, but it beats doing the wrong thing!

Timesaving Tip 3 – if you have forgotten to ask a question or don't understand something, check with a colleague or a secretary.

The secretary may know how the partner likes their research assignments. The colleague may have a good precedent you can rely upon. The colleague may know the litigation and know what jurisdiction you should be doing the research in. It beats immediately barging in like an idiot.

Timesaving Tip 4 – don't ask questions in a stream of consciousness.

If you don't understand the instructions, or you have struck a problem, don't charge into the partner's office with a question. Good partners and senior lawyers are happy to answer questions, but a junior lawyer who comes into the office 10 times to ask 10 questions on one document taxes the partner/senior lawyer's patience and destroys their concentration. Rather when you have a question, write it down. Think about it. Potentially move onto another part of the document (where you will no doubt have other questions). Write them down. Think about the logical answer. Once you have the 10 questions about the document that you need answered, go in to the partner's office, explain that you will need 5 minutes, and ask those questions. In short, don't show up 10 times at a senior lawyer's door when you could have only shown up once.

Timesaving tip 5 – don't be too eager

We get it. You are keen, enthusiastic and looking for work. That doesn't mean that you need to walk around three times a day asking for work. It throws the concentration of senior lawyers and partners out, and pretty soon you they will dislike you for wasting their time and be even less willing to give you work. A better strategy might be checking in on a daily basis when you first start but otherwise focus on building relationships with people and building your legal skills and reputation so that you are front of mind when they get a new task.

Lesson 5 – be precise and careful

Lawyers are paid, or at least are charged out for, a lot of money. Clients of BigLaw expect high standards. Your internal clients (senior lawyers and partners) expect the same high standards. If you are imprecise in your work, or aren't careful, the senior lawyers and partners will not trust you. Always re-read your work and spell-check it before giving it to a partner. Always sweat the details – check the citations, double-proofread your work, review the work of others and you'll be loved by partners in no time.

I was once on a large discovery project with about 10 lawyers to determine what documents to discover and what to claim privilege. Part of my job was to review samples of documents reviewed by the junior lawyers to make sure they were doing the work correctly. One of the junior lawyers, who clearly thought discovery was beneath them, wasn't paying attention in discovery and marked as discoverable a number of documents that were clearly privileged. Three things arose with that:

- This lawyer made a basic error arising from lack of care. How could I trust them to continue to work on that project, or any other project? There is no way I had the time to review every piece of work they did from then on to ensure that they hadn't missed anything else.
- This lawyer had 'reviewed' a large number of other documents. If they missed something this obvious, what else could they have missed? What could happen if we disclosed privileged material to the other side because of their errors?
- I had to tell my partner about the issue. Thankfully we were ahead of schedule and were able to get another junior lawyer to come in and re-review those documents (with this time being written off naturally). By this point myself, my partner,

and a number of members of the team would never work with this lawyer again, and indeed the junior lawyer left the firm shortly afterwards.

We were lucky, we had the time and resources to review their errors and fix their work. In many cases that isn't the case. Due diligence works on a very tight timeline and generally there is little time to double review documents. At the minimum, the senior lawyer managing the due diligence would have sleepless nights knowing that they had a careless lawyer prone to making errors on their hands. At the worst the wrong document would be disclosed, or failed to be disclosed, or failed to be brought to the client's attention, which could derail a large transaction and cause a malpractice suit. Being careful matters, and a careless associate is not a trusted associate.

Lesson 6 – use your brain

You are one of the brightest minds in your generation, or so your mother/graduating speaker told you. You may not know anything about practicing law, but you can still use your brain. This doesn't mean taking the initiative with a transaction or piece of litigation. It means solving the problem that comes up before you without wasting everyone else's time. Here are a couple of things that really annoy senior lawyers that could really have been solved by using a brain!

Don't blindly follow instructions

Senior lawyers aren't perfect, but a good junior lawyer should be able to read (or at least attempt to read) their mind. For example, if a partner, when giving you his edits on a 80 page document, changes the name of a defined term in the definitions and then in the first instance, you should be smart enough to know to change it elsewhere in the document. Ditto if you are re-working an affidavit, only the affidavit was prepared a while ago when the parties to the proceedings had different names—take the initiative and change the names of the parties in the re-worked affidavit. If you have been asked to make changes to a document and identify an obvious error in the document (and I mean obvious, e.g. the cross-reference is wrong, the party name is wrong, the date is wrong), fix it yourself and don't simply let it slide.

Don't tell the senior lawyer that there is a problem without thinking through the problem and offering a viable solution

This is especially the case with something that is not substantive. If the automatic cross-referencing in the document has broken down, don't tell the partner that it has broken down and expect them to do something. Call helpdesk or the word processing operator and see if they can provide a solution. Then either fix it yourself, or go to the partner and say 'By the way, the cross-referencing has broken down, the WP is free and will take about an hour to fix it, do you mind if I give it to him/her'. See it really wasn't that hard.

Equally even for matters that verge on the substantive, at least think through the problem and offer a solution, i.e. 'the case that we relied upon in this submission is no longer good law. It has been overturned by x v y which said …. Here is a copy of the case for your review. Would you like me to go through the submissions and highlight the areas in which we rely on this case so we are aware of what we may need to redraft? If you agree with me that x v y overturns our case let me know and I'll draft a short e-mail to the client with the case'. At least there you are using your brains and initiative and not dumping problem in a senior lawyer's lap without even the possibility of a solution.

Don't blindly follow the precedent

Precedents are great. They save you from having to do too much thinking and ensure that the document you produce fits in with the way the firm wants it to be done. However, if the firm wanted junior lawyers to essentially put names, dates and figures in precedents they would have the secretaries do the work. In short, don't blindly follow the precedent with no regard for the current matter. If you are that dumb, and are called on it, simply saying that the 'precedent said so' will not win you points with your partners.

If you are asked to draft originating process for litigation and the precedent is for claims a, b, and c, but your actual claim is b, c, and d, turning up with a document that keeps claim a and doesn't include d indicates to the partner that either:

- you know or understand nothing about the case; or
- you simply didn't have your brain switched on.

That doesn't do much for your reputation. Know what you have been asked to do and if the precedent doesn't match either change it yourself, or check with the senior lawyer ('this precedent is for claims a, b and c, while our case is for b, c and d, are you happy for me to delete the section that relates to a and add a section that relates to d').

Lesson 7 - don't deliver drafts to your partner/senior lawyer

Senior Lawyers are busy and don't have time to correct spelling mistakes, grammar or check citations. It annoys them no end and it looks like you have been careless. Before you give any work to a senior lawyer, proofread it twice and correct any error. If you hand up a well-written piece of work you'll look good. If you hand up a piece of work with the wrong client's name on it, you will look like an untrustworthy fool, regardless of the brilliance of your legal thinking.

If you are in a situation where you want to go down a legal rabbit hole (a new argument in an advice for example), but don't want to start serious work on the argument until you discuss it with a partner, discuss it with a partner – don't deliver a half-finished piece of work that partly raises the argument. If the partner is unavailable, send them an e-mail and follow up. If they still don't reply, either do the work with the new argument, or send them a perfect bit of work without the argument, only with a cover e-mail explaining what you think you should do.

The only exception to the rule is in circumstances where you are under extreme time pressure. You need to get an advice out within the hour. You have found someone else's work on the firm's system and have cut and pasted it into a document and given it to the partner to review before they speak to a client. It may not be perfect but it is the best you can do at short notice. Partners understand that sometimes things need to be done urgently but don't get into the habit of shortcuts.

Lesson 8 - don't take too much initiative

Junior lawyers should use their brain. That doesn't mean ignoring the instructions because you think there is a better way of doing things. There is a reason the senior lawyer is senior and has given you instructions to do it a particular way: they either know what they are doing or they want it done a particular way.

If you decide that you want to structure a document differently, or prepare a client summary in a different way, or (and you'd be really stupid to try this without checking) prepare originating process for a different cause of action/in a different court, then please check with the senior lawyer. It's not hard to go in and say 'I've had a think about this and I think we should do it this way because.' At least then the senior lawyer is in a position to hear your argument and respond. There may be a good reason why the senior lawyer wants it done that way that you don't appreciate (the partner likes it that way, the client has a preference, there is a legal reason why this has to be done). What is stupid is to simply take the initiative, deviate from the instructions, and then, at the deadline when the senior lawyer is expecting x, delivering y. If you are right and y is the way to go, the senior lawyer will be annoyed that you didn't tell him/her first. If you are wrong, suddenly either you or the senior lawyer has to re-draft the document under deadline pressure. Either way, if you don't communicate early with the senior lawyer, you look very bad.

This is particularly egregious when dealing with clients. You may not deal with clients directly much in your early years, or you may have some reasonable contacts. If there is an issue and you decide to 'take the initiative' and respond to clients directly, you better be damn certain that you are right, and that you have expressed yourself in a professional, client-friendly way. If you are legally incorrect, have contradicted the partner, have written something incoherent, or are otherwise wrong, you have hugely embarrassed yourself in front of the partner and client. Do you think the client wants to pay your hourly rate for a cowboy?

Lesson 9 - don't be in the wrong place at the wrong time

Sometimes good lawyers get fired. They are in an area of the law firm that the managing partners decide to get rid of. They are in an area that is heavily cyclical (try being a securitization lawyer post-2008), and are let go because they have no work. Their supervising partner retired and the team was let go following that. The firm failed or the office was shut down.

This happens and I hope it doesn't happen to you. Obviously you have used your spidey sense to try and find a way to keep your job and it hasn't happened. Hopefully this has happened at a time the market is good, and you have a reasonable range of options, but here are some useful tips if it does all go wrong.

- Try and make it to the two year mark at your firm. You become much more employable at that point. Every firm that employs graduate lawyers already has them, and no firm that doesn't want graduates is interested in recruiting someone of one year's experience.
- On the same note, see if the firm will let you stay with them, or at least retain access to their e-mail address and facilities

for the purpose of getting a new job. You become much more employable if you are still 'working' in a firm.

- If your entire team is getting the sack, stay close to the partner. Partners move firms all the time and take team members (or favorite team members) with them. If you partner is nice, then they'll try and put their team in the lifeboat. If they aren't, they'll only put his favorite team members. Make sure you are one of them.

- If you were fired for reasons other than your incompetence, try and get written references to this effect. Ideally ones that clearly say that [name] was an excellent performer who was let go due to a staffing oversupply/decision to eliminate his team. There is a risk that people will perceive you as having been fired because you were 'difficult' or didn't get the work done. Try to set yourself up to show that this isn't the case (even consider including these references in future applications). If your partner/team leader is a good person in a firm going through problems they'll give you an excellent written reference.

Chapter 3 - Social functions

Every BigLaw firm insists—as a matter of team-building or client building—on numerous social activities. Whether it be drinks on the floor with the team, monthly drinks at a nearby bar, a wild and over-the-top Christmas Party, or a formal dinner when the great and the good of the firm give speeches, it seems like there are never-ending opportunities to wine and dine on the firm's tab.

Social opportunities are divided into two categories—external events (i.e. with clients and other lawyers) and internal events (within the firm) and their role should be treated separately.

Lesson 1 – internal events don't matter that much

Now I'm sure you have read some useful advice about networking and realize the importance of making your mark with key people at the firm. See that M&A partner—go over there and talk about the big deal they did. See the managing partner—go over there and introduce yourself to him/her and complement him/her on the fine work the firm is doing. You're going straight to the top!

In the real world, we have words for people like that—gunners, brown-nosers and the annoyingly pushy. It may work, but it is transparent and the important person may either not remember your name or remember the name of the annoying little junior lawyer who got me in a really boring conversation when they was trying to relax after a big week.

There are two questions about firm social events 1) should you go and 2) what should you do there?

Should you go?

The answer is if you want to go, then go. If you have better things to do, don't go. Unless you have specifically been ordered to attend a particular event (which sometime applies to firm formal dinners), social events are voluntary. Realistically, while you might miss out on a networking opportunity, the same can be said for missing a

CLE, not arriving at the firm early enough, not going out for coffee, or skipping legal events. You lead a busy life. If you want to spend time with your family and friends, or just sleep just do so. Nobody has ever been fired for not attending sufficient social events.

What should you do there?

Once you have decided that the lure of free beer and snacks is sufficient to drag you out of your office to said social event, what's the best strategy for making the most of your time there?

My personal view is the best thing you can do is have a few drinks, relax and have some fun. You work hard enough as it is. You need some time to blow off steam and have a good time with your work friends. Have fun. Talk about work if you want, but feel free to talk about anything else. Flirt with that attractive lawyer you have your eye on (but don't take it any further on-site, and be careful). If you happen to run into a partner, have a chat and treat them like a human being. They are trying to blow off steam too.

If you want to be more strategic about your approach to social functions, a good strategy is this: Make friends with people in different teams and catch up with old friends who are now in different teams. Your career will be improved with a good network of contacts, otherwise known as friends. That lawyer you started with in M&A but haven't seen for a while; in 10 years s/he could be legal counsel at a big client. That senior associate who you talked football with; they could be a partner down the track reviewing your application for partnership. You may not work in their areas but you never know when your friends may be useful. It is certainly more fun than mechanically 'networking' with people and sending LinkedIn invitations. Those contacts are rarely helpful but good friends in the profession are. Plus they can share great gossip about who is good and bad to work with and what else is going on with the firm.

In terms of bad behavior at firm functions, try not to do anything stupid in your summer associateship/first few months. Once you have been at the firm for a while, and have a reasonable reputation, firms have a fair degree of tolerance for stupid behavior in firm functions (I can assure you that you won't be the first person who has vomited at a Christmas party, or spilled a drink on a partner, or set off the firm sprinklers), but try and limit the risk. Here are my tips:

- Know your drinking limits. You can get drunk but not stupidly drunk. Know your tolerance, and what you are like when you've had a few drinks and moderate.
- Don't do anything illegal. Don't do drugs on firm property, steal stuff from a function, or otherwise commit vandalism. If you are the sort of person who does this after a few drinks, then don't drink at functions
- Keep your racist, sexist and homophobic comments to yourself. You may be among friends at a firm function. You may be doing it ironically. Your impression of a Chinese judge may be legitimately hilarious, but you don't know who is around you and who could be insulted. Is a laugh really worth, at the minimum, a trip to HR, and a severe talking-to by your partner.
- Don't follow up a firm social function by having sex in your office. Yes it happens. Yes you'll be a legend and have a great story to embarrass your kids with, but the risk isn't worth it. Regardless of your gender you don't want the reputation as the office sleaze. You don't want to be caught. You don't want to have to deal with a HR complaint or worse if it goes wrong. If you and your sexual partner aren't the exact same level of seniority you don't want the creepy office politics vibe. In short, if you see a hottie at a law firm, be classy like Barack and Michelle: go on a date outside the office.

Lesson 2 - external functions are part of your job so treat it like a job

External functions are a harder case. To some degree they are part of the job and should be treated that way, while other functions can be easier to blow off.

Firstly if your partner asks you to come to an external function, you should come. It is part of your job.

If the function is optional, and you are a very junior lawyer, you can get away with missing it, but there is some virtue in coming, meeting a few people, and watching how the senior members of the team operate. This is where networking is useful and you have to learn it sometime. As a more senior lawyer you'll be going to a lot more client functions, so you might as well build some relationships now.

As for non-client functions, bar association functions and the like, it depends on the function. You should probably try and meet a few people, but realistically you lead a busy life and missing a few functions won't kill you.

Unlike firm functions, you should be on your best behavior. You're representing the firm and embarrassing behavior at a client or external function will affect your future prospects. Your partner might think you are a great lawyer, but if the clients don't like working with you, or they can't trust you to spend time with clients without embarrassing yourself, you are of little use to them.

Chapter 4 – Seminars – are they really a complete waste of time?

One of the banes of any lawyer's existence in BigLaw is the seemingly never ending list of lunchtime and after-work seminars that one gets invited to. There are several rules as to when to go and when to skip the seminars.

Lesson 1 - if the seminar is necessary for you to remain qualified to practice law, go.

This is the most obvious rule, but one that is necessary. Track your CLE points (or ask your secretary to do so) and make sure you don't have issues staying qualified in your jurisdiction.

Lesson 2 - if your partner tells you to go, then go

It is part of your job.

Lesson 3 - for anything else, either take it seriously or don't go

I have been to hundreds of legal seminars, listening to partners or other lawyers drone on about legal matters of dubious relevance to my practice. Most of that information has gone straight through my head, as well as the heads of other lawyers attending. Meanwhile, at the front of the room, notebook in hand, was one of my firm's most senior partners who took diligent notes at every seminar. There is a reason why he was a legend of the firm, a lawyer's lawyer, and why I'm writing this book.

Either take a seminar seriously, or don't bother going. If you want to take the seminar seriously, sit at the front, take a notepad, take detailed notes, and try and file away the knowledge or handouts generated by the seminar. If you want to skip it, there are plenty of more productive things to do with your time (billable work, exercise, lunch with a friend). The worst option is do what most lawyers do. Grab the free lunch and doze in the back of the room for an hour. It won't make you a better lawyer, it won't improve your career, and it won't make you happy. You have a tough, demanding job. Use your time wisely.

Lesson 4 - if you have to go, don't listen, present

Presentation skills are a vital part of becoming a good lawyer. As your career goes on, you'll need to show prospective clients that you are good confident lawyer who knows the law. It is also a way to impress more senior partners, especially if you can use a flashier piece of software than PowerPoint. They may bring you along to client meetings, get you to present at conferences and do all those little things that can help build a career. Perhaps, most importantly, if you present about an area of law you WILL learn that area of law and become a better lawyer for it.

While presenting a seminar does involve more work, it is generally worth it. You get the kudos, the legal knowledge and the opportunity to impress others. Equally, if you start presenting in your first year or two, you will make all your mistakes early, when it counts for less. You don't want to be a senior lawyer, gunning for partner, doing a CLE in front of the partners who will judge your application, yet be a person who can't present a legal CLE in an interesting and coherent way!

Chapter 5 - Dealing with Clients

Clients are of course the reason law firms exist. Partners live and die by them, they pay your wages, and it is their stuff-ups (litigation) or empire building desires (deals) that provides the work that you do.

Oddly enough, clients aren't actually that important to a junior lawyer. They are important in the meta-sense outlined above, but in the day-to-day reality of practicing law as a junior lawyer in a BigLaw firm, your client is the partner you work for, and your obligation is to impress them with your work. If you impress the client too that is great (and if this positive impression is passed on to your partner that is even better) but this is fairly rare – your job is to do the work for the partner, and the partner to impress the client.

Client contact can be divided into two circumstances; work contact and social contact.

Lesson 1 – If you are meeting the client for work purposes, your job is to make your partner look good

Your contact with a client will vary greatly in your first few years depending on the type of matters that you work on. If you are working in advisory, you may never see or hear from the client; rather you will simply get research tasks to work on. In litigation you may see the client at trials, when preparing evidence (although you may be dealing with witnesses, not clients), and at some client meetings, if your partner takes you along. In deals your client contact varies depending on the partner. Some will be happy to do all the client contact and get all the instructions, while others will delegate obtaining instructions in respect of particular issues (especially in relation to technical questions, such as the acceptance of a particular clause in a contract) to you. There are a couple of broad tips:

In client meetings with your partner, your job is to make your boss look good

This means:

- smiling and shaking hands
- taking clear and copious notes and potentially sending a summary to everyone afterwards (depending on partner instructions); and
- if your partner is well-prepared and on the ball, say little or nothing unless specifically asked; or
- if your partner is poorly prepared/not on top of the matter either:
  - run the meeting if instructed by your partner to do in advance (and check with your partner in advance if they want you to take the lead); or
  - gently prompt the partner regarding particular issues on the matter and field questions that the partner throws to you.

Again your job is to make the partner look good. Meetings with the client are not the time to discuss your theories of the matter (the partner may need to correct you and that looks bad), or to get into an argument with your partner about strategy. To the extent you want to discuss your theories, you should have done it in advance. The key thing to remember is the golden rule: <u>Never contradict or disagree with your partner in front of the client</u>. Nothing makes the partner look more unprofessional and annoys the partner more than being contradicted by his junior. They either look stupid, or you look stupid; neither is good for client relations.

If you think the partner has done something wrong in the meeting or is mistaken in some way, don't correct him/her in front of the clients. Speak to him/her afterwards in the privacy of your office. They can always call the clients back with a 'of course when I said this, I meant to say this' phone call. Also, you may be wrong and it is better to be shown up in a partner's office than in front of the client.

If the meeting is going very wrong and the partner is giving clearly incorrect advice based on a misunderstanding of the facts (i.e. advising that a client can't be sued because of a limitation period, based on a misunderstanding of when the conduct occurred), or is clearly embarrassing himself/herself (by talking about the wrong case, or the wrong client), either:

- ask the partner a pointed question to get him/her on track (So, does the limitation period apply when the conduct took place in 2013, as was the case here?). Note the degree of difficulty level here is a 9/10; or
- apologize to the clients and ask to meet the partner outside the conference room. If the partner is right, they can always brush off your intervention as 's/he had just received an e-mail relating to another matter and wanted to check if it was urgent', and if you are right you have saved the partner from embarrassing himself/herself and your client valuable time.

If you are closely involved in the matter you should prepare for every client meeting. The partner or client (if you have been dealing closely with them), may ask you questions or may ask you to explain areas of the matter, since you are most on top of the details. Be on top of the facts of the matter and be prepared to answer those questions. In particular, be on top of to-do lists and other timeframes. It does your reputation a world of good if you can say to a client, without checking notes: 'This document needs to be completed by [date]. It is 80% ready and just needs to be reviewed by the partner. Our next task is XYZ, which we want to get done by [date]. I'll send you an e-mail by [date] seeking your input by [date] following which we will send it to the other side and ask them to respond by [date].' That shows the client (and the partner) that you are on top of their matter and makes the partner look good.

Otherwise look professional and look on top of the material. You may have other non-meeting interactions with the client. This may be at a deal signing, at a negotiation with another party, in court as part of a litigation team, or at an on-site visit. The key thing to remember is that clients (especially legal counsel) don't expect the junior lawyer to be a legal genius who has all the answers, but they do expect him/her to be professional, and on top of all the material in the matter (which is his/her job of course).

This means preparation: If you are going to court, have spare copies of every document that could possibly be needed. Know which cases are going to be needed and have copies of them available. Even if you are not speaking, be engaged in the process, so that you can tell a client what is happening at any particular time. If you are at a negotiation, have the relevant documents and know the facts of the case. The client or partner may be a better negotiator, but they may need to be prompted on the facts (that's your job). At the deal signing, have all the documents clean, tabbed and ready. Be prepared to tell the client exactly what each document is and why it needs to be signed. The important thing is that you shouldn't look like you are along for the experience and contributing nothing, rather you should look like you know what your job is (provide support, cover for everyone else) and that you are focused on doing it and providing the client with value.

Be careful with direct e-mails and phone calls with the client
Every partner is different and tolerates different levels of direct communication between their associates and their clients, but the key rule is 'be careful'. If you provide advice to a client directly and it is wrong, they can commence proceedings against your firm; something that could end your career. If you provide correct advice, but in the wrong format, style or unsuited for the present issue you may annoy your partner or the client (especially if the partner did not know what you were doing). If you provide advice that

contradicts your partner's advice (even unknowingly) you have embarrassed your partner and damaged your reputation.

So how do you minimize the risk of these things happening/maximize the trust of the partner/client? A couple of tips:

- Don't have any client communication.

Good advice, but perhaps overly-optimistic. There will be times where the partner or senior lawyer is not around or the client wants to talk with you (s/he is paying your wages after all).

- If you do have client communication, know the matter back to front

Again, good advice, but hard to perfect in the real world. Junior lawyers don't know everything.

- If you communicate in e-mail and it is at all substantive (i.e. not something a secretary could have said), run it by the partner or senior lawyer.

This is broadly good practice unless the partner specifically makes it clear that they don't need to see everything. If the advice is time-pressured (i.e. you have to get it out by x) and the partner doesn't go through his inbox frequently, then either talk to his secretary to see if s/he can put it in front of him/her or run it past a more senior lawyer. Don't do the 'I gave it to you at 9, and didn't receive a response by 3 so I sent it out'. Partners are overworked and sometimes don't see something unless it is put in front of them.

- If you communicate by phone, either send an e-mail recording what you said, or draft a file-note.

Again, you have a record of what you said in case there is any issue later on. I am notorious for sending e-mails to myself recording the contents of phone conversations, as they are easily stored, difficult to lose and clearly time and date stamped in the event that they become relevant later on.

- If you must have a communication with a client on a substantive matter without the partner or a senior lawyer, try and limit it to the receipt of instructions and or the provision of information, but not the provision of legal advice.

You aren't paid to give legal advice to clients. Partners are paid to provide legal advice to clients, because they know the law and have the practical experience. You are paid to provide your unsophisticated opinion to them and they can decide whether to pass it on to clients. When speaking directly to clients, or sending e-mails, try as much as possible to limit it to passing on facts (' please find attached document x. The other side has made substantive changes at y, z and a. You may wish to know that in our last transaction with the other side they accepted our drafting at y and z, but insisted on their position in a. Please let me have your instructions as to whether we should accept their changes.') and requesting instructions.

- If you must provide advice to a client, and the partner/senior lawyer is unavailable; provide the advice but with significant caveats.

A client should know better than ask a lawyer with 1 years' experience whether to accept the other side's changes in a document, or whether an additional affidavit needs to be prepared in a matter. If the client asks, you should always try and run it past a senior lawyer; however if the client directly asks your advice, or you aren't in a position to get assistance, assist the client to the best of your ability, but make it clear the limited basis you provide your advice, i.e. 'My opinion is that you should accept their substantive change in x. In the event of a default, your position is protected in y, however you should be aware that I have only worked in this area for 1 year, and I don't have the same experience as [partner]. His advice may differ from mine and he will be available at [time]. Would you like me to run this by him/her when he/she is available and contact you to confirm his view of the matter.' Then record this conversation by sending an e-mail or a file-note. You have helped the client and the client is fully aware of the limited nature of the advice provided, and a lawsuit against the firm on the basis that the client took the advice of a junior lawyer that s/he was aware was provisional is unlikely to succeed.

At the same time, if the advice sought is outside your expertise, or is couched in general terms, don't try and assist the client by providing your best guess as to what they should do. This is particularly the case when dealing with in less sophisticated clients, or when the clients aren't legal counsel as they may misinterpret the limited advice provided by a terrified junior lawyer. If the client comes to you and says 'should I send out this e-mail or am I at risk of defamation?' don't say 'it looks fine to me'. Say either 'I'll run it by my partner', or 'I'm sorry, I don't know enough about the facts of the case and/or defamation law to give you any reasonable advice in this matter. I'd be doing you a disservice by telling you that you should or should not send it, as I don't have the expertise to assist here.' You may annoy the client, who might be looking for a more 'can-do' lawyer but you may also have saved your firm from an embarrassing lawsuit or a grumpy client.

Provide recommendations and solutions, not problems

Similar to any advice you would give your partner, if you are giving advice to a client, don't just throw a problem in their lap and let them deal with it. If there is a legal issue with what the client is trying to do, clearly identify the issue and provide some solutions for the client to consider. Your options may not be the one the client actually picks (the client knows more than you) but they will be impressed with the fact that as a lawyer, you are actually trying to help them, instead of making life more miserable.

You'll get better and more experienced with clients as you become more senior.

The advice above is targeted at very junior lawyers who don't have the expertise in the law and dealing with clients. Once you become more senior you start understanding your individual clients, what they need to know, and how to provide them with advice. Your partner will start trusting you more with running meetings and interacting with clients without running things past him/her. In short things will get better: But as a junior lawyer, remember to be very, very careful with client interactions, as you simply don't have the experience or judgment to make more than the simplest of calls with or in front of a client.

Lesson 2 - In social situations, the aim is to make the partner look good (and not embarrass yourself)

The partner is taking the client's legal team out to dinner and as the brilliant junior lawyer, you have been invited along (or you are just there to make up the numbers because an actual important lawyer passed). It may be a fun night; the drinks may be flowing, but you have one job—don't screw up. Don't do anything that could lose the client.

Generally clients are pretty good people socially. If you are dealing with legal counsel; they are often ex-BigLaw people, so they will have been in your position, will know the drill and are really interested in having a good time. If you are dealing with business people; they may be a bit more enthusiastic about the business, but again are social enough (the ones who are socially awkward tend not to come to these functions).

So, how can you avoid embarrassing yourself at a client function? A lot of the circumstances below are not sackable offences (a client is unlikely to fire a partner because a junior lawyer who is in the team 6 months got drunk at a function), but are is still things to avoid.

- Don't talk about ongoing matters unless asked! Most clients are there for a good time and don't need to be bored by their lawyer discussing only their existing matters. Try and stick to safe topics to start with – family, sports, travel etc. Alternatively, if you don't know about the client's business ask them about it: what are their major issues, what are the legal risks, how do they differentiate themselves from competitors. Clients love to talk about themselves, love having someone who is interested in them, and who knows, it may even help you serve their interests!
- If they do want to discuss ongoing matters, by all means discuss them, but never say anything that could be constituted as a criticism of the partner or suggest that you disagree with anything the partner says. Your job at a law firm, both in your work and socially is to make your partner look good. Don't be self-deprecating about your work and if you want to display your sense of humor, target it at the other side and their pomposities, but be careful.
- Display some knowledge about the client, and some understanding of their business, even if it is something you don't agree with. You don't want to be the lawyer who informed their client, a pharmaceutical corporation, that 's/he didn't know what brands of drugs they produced because s/he only used generic drugs'.
- Be careful with client true believers; i.e. the one that has drunk the company Kool-Aid. Most company employees (and this is especially true of legal counsel) respect their employer, but don't think they are the greatest company in the world. Apple people accept that some people prefer Microsoft products. United employees wouldn't necessarily fly their own airline, and Toyota people might prefer Fords, just like any fair minded lawyer would understand that there are other firms that practice law totally respectably. However, each company has their share of true believers,

who fervently believe that United is the world's greatest airline, that Samsung does produce the best mobile phones (and will judge you if you use an iPhone), that Coke does taste better than Pepsi, so if you happen to be with one of them, be respectful and courteous. You don't need to fervently agree with them, just respect their position, and don't do anything obnoxiously rude (like order an American wine in front of a true believing representative of a French wine company).

- Don't be seriously drunk, boorish or insulting. Many a client relationship has been sealed in a bar over a few beers. However this is something a senior lawyer should do. A junior lawyer who drinks too much is unlikely to bond with a client sufficiently to help the partner, and risks embarrassing the partner and the client, who may not trust someone who doesn't know how to behave in an adult situation. The best advice for drinking at a client function is either do very little of it or (if you are a regular drinker) match the client drink for drink but never go past them.

Chapter 6 - Other things I wished I had known starting out in BigLaw

Lesson 1 - There is often no real right or wrong, but only what the partner wants you to do

Even in large law firms, partners are not homogenous. They have different temperaments, different ways of working, and different ways of receiving information. Frequently, there are issues in which there is no obvious right or wrong and partners in the same firm can take different positions on the same issue. Your job is to do what your partner wants you to do.

For example, if you are working in a transactional firm, Partner A might take the position that a certain guarantee in a type of finance contract is completely market standard and is happy to recommend to his client to agree to such a clause in any contract they sign. Partner B may take the completely opposite position and come to the view that the guarantee is unfair, not market and would never recommend to his client to agree to such a clause. You move from Partner A to partner B and get chewed out for agreeing to such a guarantee in the contract. It's not your fault: just grin and bear it and don't make the same mistake next time.

Equally, partners take different approaches as to how close they monitor their staff's work. You might have done one deal with Partner A, who doesn't need to see every draft before it goes to the other side. You start a new deal with Partner B, who chews you out for that conduct. Again, grin and bear it and don't make the same mistake next time.

Lesson 2 – Researchers and WP operators are nature's gifts to junior lawyers

Not all firms employ specialist researches but if you are in a firm that does, use them. This varies by firm but in my experience anyone employed by a firm as a specialist legal researcher is amazing. Your own research skills may be limited to what you did in Law School or have atrophied in your first few years, but their skills are sharp as ever. They are also up to date with the latest research technology and can be far more efficient than you ever could. Even if you don't get them to do your work, a 5 minute chat at the beginning of your research task could save you hours and give you a whole new suite of research tools. They are worthwhile befriending as soon as possible.

Equally important are the WP or helpdesk operators. Again, not all firms have word processing operators and they are increasingly being outsourced, but if you can, know how to use these wonderful people and what they do. BigLaw firms work on precedents and precedents, especially for long documents, can break down easily. If your precedent is showing problems (i.e. wording is moving, cross-references aren't working, you are getting gibberish, these are the people you need to fix it. By the way, precedents always break down between 10pm and 3am, so if your firm has one or more night WP operators or helpdesk people, these are the ones to befriend.

Lesson 3 - HR people are not your friends

Human resources staff aren't bad people. They do lots of warm and fuzzy things around the law firm (look at our white partner lecture a sea of non-white associates! Aren't we diverse!) They also work to drive some change in law firm offerings to keep up with the market, including improved maternity leave policies and some improved support for lawyers with work/life balance issues. They can also inform management if they are legally in the wrong on a particular issue.

However, whenever you deal with an HR person, remember who s/he works for: the partners. Remember who decides whether s/he gets promoted or fired: the partners. Don't disclose anything to a HR person that you wouldn't be happy being reported to the partners.

Lesson 4 – It gets better

The first few years at a law firm can be really tough. The hours are brutal, the work is full of boring/menial/repetitive work, and you are often completely out of your depth (We need to send out this document in the next 30 mins and I can't find the partner. What do I do?).

It gets better.

I'm not encouraging you to stay at a law firm if you are really unhappy, but I'm just telling you that the practice of law as a 4th or 6th year lawyer is much more interesting, comfortable, and enjoyable than as a junior lawyer. Not in all ways, but in many important ways.

It gets better because:

Work gets more interesting

It really does. In year one you are doing endless research tasks and/or editing and amending documents on the instructions of other lawyers. No matter how exciting it is wearing a suit and working in the big city, the glamour of being the person who sits on a conference call to take notes (and for some partners that means verbatim transcripts) goes away quickly.

By the time you get to be a 4th year associate, you are reviewing and editing someone else's research memos and considering suggestions to improve them. You are part of strategy meetings, where you actually discuss how the litigation/deal will be planned out. You might be asked your opinion on something. In conference calls, you may still be taking notes, or you may be participating but the difference is that you actually understand what is going on. You start seeing the big picture of what the client is trying to achieve, and the role of the law firm in getting the best outcome and the steps that need to be taken. You understand the elements of a transaction, how litigation works, what laws cover what. Practicing law starts to somewhat resemble what you thought lawyers did back at law school.

The learning curve is less steep

The first six months of legal practice are exciting and terrifying. Everything you do will be doing something for the first time. The first transaction. The first all-nighter. The first time you go to court. The first time you call another lawyer to discuss the case (and yes, every new lawyer spends 15 mins planning the call just in case the other lawyer decides to get into a detailed discussion of the legal issues). It's terrifying.

By year 4 you are still learning. Every deal or case is different. Every day you are confronted with a different problem. However, there are some things you do know and are fairly relaxed about. You can call another lawyer at another firm to chat about a matter. You are comfortable calling a client. You know when to get someone more senior involved and what matters you can handle yourself. You know how to draft a letter, draft an affidavit, draft a transaction document and can review the work of others. In short, on most days you go into work knowing that you can competently handle most of what is thrown your way and are unlikely to get fired.

You can delegate/don't have to do boring/menial/repetitive work

Due diligence, discovery, reading documents out loud to each other, printing out hundreds of pages of documents for a signing: all of these tasks are ones that you are now far too senior or important for. Sure you might be reviewing the work of others, or decide to do an hour of discovery just to keep your hand in, but your work is interesting and challenging, not mind-numbing and detail-oriented.

The exception to the rule is editing and reviewing. You'll be doing a lot of it. That means fixing up the work of others, and reviewing their changes to documents. You may not like it but it beats the hell out of due diligence.

You know how to work with your partner/partners

You've been in the game a while now, Ms. not-a-junior-lawyer anymore. If you work for a single partner you'll have been working for them for a few years now. If you work for multiple partners and senior lawyers, you'll have probably been on a few matters now with most of them and if not, at least know how they operate/know people who know how they operate. This doesn't mean you'll be perfect but at least:

- You know when and how to bother them;
- You know how they like to receive their work (written, with/without tracking, by e-mail, not at all etc.);
- You know what their pet peeves are (spelling, grammar, lateness, whether or not you can answer their legal questions etc.);
- You know how they like to run their matters and what degree of supervision they give (i.e. what do you need to run past them? If they have done one review, do you need to give them another?); and
- Possibly most importantly, you know their flaws. Some partners are useless before 10am, some useless after 10pm. Some have horrible tempers (and you know to check with their secretary before seeing them), others have no sense of humor. Some are average lawyers (so you should check the law before drafting advice based on their statements), while others are great lawyers but terrible detail people (so make sure you review the junior lawyer's work because the partner will sign anything).

So much of law firm practice is dealing with the partners, and after a few years the terror and misunderstandings stop, and are replaced by a healthy understanding of their strengths and flaws and what needs to be done to work with them.

You know how to work with your secretary (and him/her with you)

The first interactions with secretaries are never easy. You were told what they were supposed to do, but can you really actually tell that person what to do? But s/he works with two other people much more senior to you, will s/he ever do your work? Anyway, short of going to McDonalds, you've never given commands to anyone anyway.

By your 4th year, you've risen up the pecking order, and so secretaries will actually do your work. You also are comfortable giving clear commands to your secretary ('I've just sent you an e-mail. Can you please print out all the attachments 3 times and prepare 3 folders with tables of contents to give to myself, x and y by 10am tomorrow. Thanks very much and let me know if you are having any problems.') You'll also know your secretary's capabilities. Is s/he able to do your filing? Can s/he draft basic cover letters? Is s/he only good for being on Facebook and participating in long phone calls? S/he will also know how you like to do your work (are you happy for him/her to handle all the paper files or do you do your own filing? Do you maintain your own calendar or are you happy for your secretary to do it for you?) These things just make the practice of law a little bit easier and a little bit less stressful.

You have a reputation (which means you can take liberties)

Assuming you have taken the sterling lessons in this book, you have a reputation around the firm as a competent, hard-working lawyer. You've done a few all-nighters, and impressed a few people. People know they can trust you, know that you don't let things slip, and know that if you say something will be done, it will get done. This sort of reputation is what you spend your early years building.

What that means is that you can take liberties. If things are quiet, and you need to go out on a two hour hair appointment, you can (as long as you inform everyone). You can slip out to the gym for a workout. I had colleagues in deals who immediately after sending documents to the other side (knowing that they won't have anything else to do for 8 hours), would go and watch a movie. As long as your partner knows where you are and knows that you can and will get the work done, taking these liberties won't damage your reputation. Equally, if you tell a partner that you'll get a document to him/her at 9am and then promptly go home, s/he's unlikely to get worried, as s/he would with a junior lawyer, rather s/he trusts that you will work on it at home or come in early the next morning. You might ask if you could work from home, or if you could take half a day off at short notice. You're a trusted and valuable member of the team now and management will try and assist you when they can.

As a junior lawyer you are building your reputation, which means you can't take liberties. Not only do you not want the reputation of being a malingerer, you don't have the experience to know when to take liberties (perhaps you don't realize that the other side always calls back 1 hour after you give them the documents to seek an explanation for the changes). It is only once you get a bit more senior that you know how and when to relax, and can get away with it. Enjoy yourself!

You know your way around the firm (and who is and isn't to be trusted)

As a junior lawyer, you are often reliant on first impressions. That pioneering minority partner who is charismatic and charming. The grumpy old fossil partner. The of counsel/special counsel who is never going to be made up. The friendly secretary.

Once you have been around for a while, you may discover that the pioneering partner is a nightmare to work with. The special counsel is a font of knowledge and is perfectly happy where they are. The grumpy old fossil partner is in fact grumpy and old with no redeeming features. The friendly secretary is incompetent.

Even if you work in a large law firm and don't know everyone, you should have friends in most of the firm's groups who know what is going on. If you've just added a tax lawyer to your deals team, a quick call to a friend will confirm whether s/he knows his/her stuff. If you've gotten a transfer from another group, you can find out the reason they were transferred. In short you know the people you want to deal with, know who you don't want to deal with, and have the ability to minimize the time spent with the latter.

Lesson 5 – It doesn't get better

Some things don't get better. If the things below concern you, then you should be aware that they don't get better the more senior you become, and consider whether you really want to stay in BigLaw.

The hours don't get better

You should have worked this out. The hours don't get better. When you've been stuck in the office late at night on a deal, you would have seen plenty of more senior lawyers in the office with you. Somebody has to supervise the junior lawyers, do the complex work that they can't do and generally keep the firm running. That is the more senior non-partner lawyers. Just because you can delegate menial/boring/repetitive work doesn't mean that there isn't plenty more work left back in your office for you to do.

Also, there are other pressures that force more senior lawyers to work longer hours. They may have higher billable hour targets (some firms give consideration to junior lawyers who are just starting out and have a lot of learning to do). They may be under pressure to boost their reputation and do more work with different partners to boost their long term partnership prospects. For more senior, partnership-track lawyers, they have to spend a significant amount of time off site doing client development, as well as building their reputation within the firm, managing all their matters and maintaining their billables. While partners have more flexibility in how they manage their practice (and BigLaw partners who have managed to build successful practices while not working brutal hours do exist), the vast majority work very, very hard. In short if you want good working hours, don't stay in BigLaw.

The work-life balance doesn't get better

Many junior lawyers, fresh out of law school are single/childless/with no carer responsibilities. They make good money in their first few years and it is quite possible to live a fairly low-maintenance life (short-ish commutes, limited out-of-office commitments, a social life that revolves around the firm), that enables them to work BigLaw hours.

For most people, this changes. People get married, people have kids and parents get old and need to be looked after. People trade a longer commute for a nicer house in the suburbs. People make friends with non-lawyers. The only thing that doesn't change (or gets worse) is the working hours. It is not easy juggling all the various commitments of middle-age along with a very demanding job. While you make a good living and can outsource many of your caring responsibilities, many a lawyer has questioned why s/he is working long hours to pay for someone else to raise their children! Unless you are very lucky, combining practice with raising children will involve conference calls with your children crying in the background, missing sporting events for big deals, and hours spent at the laptop at home, reviewing documents and sending e-mails once your children go to bed. It can be done and is done by many BigLaw lawyers but if you are likely to have children, talk to the more senior lawyers in your firm about how they manage their jobs and children and decide early whether you can or want to handle the pressures they are under. If you can't/won't that's fine, but you should start considering a strategy to get out.

Your social life around the firm doesn't get better

For all the down-side, being a junior lawyer is actually pretty fun. You'll have a decent sized graduate intake in your firm. You'll bond with the rest of the intake and hopefully make a couple of really good friends. There are usually a number of social events for your graduate intake, and you'll see them at CLE events. Also if you summered at the firm you'll have a social network within your summer associate group (to the extent that they are not in your graduate group) and the groups/teams you summer associated in. Finally if your firm has rotations in different groups, you'll meet people and make friends in those groups. Drinks on a Friday night are always an option, and (if that is your interest) there are usually attractive, single members of the opposite sex (or the same sex) who are available. It beats working in a graveyard!

Five years down the track and things have gotten a lot worse. You have spent the last 4 years working in a single team for one or a few different partners. Most days you probably talk to the same 5-10 people working around you. Of your graduate class, most of them (including all your cool friends) have left the firm. Equally, of the friends you made when you rotated into other groups 4 years ago, most of them have left the firm. Every 6 months or a year you get a new fresh faced group of graduate lawyers or summer associates, who are far too intimidated by you to become good friends. Unlike as a grad, where you turned up to every CLE and caught up with friends there, you are far too busy for most CLEs (and only go if you are presenting or are short of credit). The attraction of firm social events has dimmed for you, and for your intake group, so if you do show your face, you'll be horrified at how few people there you actually know. Your lunches are generally spent at the desk, reviewing your e-mail, and if you do go out for lunch, it is part of client development. You have outside commitments which mean that your aim is to come to the office, get through the work as quickly as possible and then get out. There are still attractive, single lawyers around the firm, but most of them are much more junior than you and you don't want to risk a harassment issue arising, or even being 'the creepy guy' or 'the slutty cougar'. You may work in the same firm, but when you do encounter your good friend who works on a different floor, most of the discussion is about how long it has been since you have seen each other, and unspecified promises about catching up more often.

This isn't necessarily a bad thing. You're an adult. A job doesn't have to be joyful, or involve hanging around your friends all day. You may be quite satisfied with your work and simply want to get through it as efficiently as possible to maximize time with your family/sleep. However if one of the reasons you are staying at the firm as a junior lawyer is because of your friends there, be warned, it doesn't get better.

You have more responsibility and sometimes more stress

As a junior lawyer, you have one overarching responsibility – to get your work done and do it well. You have fairly discrete tasks, most of which can be done by hard work, using your brain, attention to detail and asking for the right assistance at the right time. As a more senior lawyer you have the responsibility to get a job done, in which the work is shared by you and that of junior lawyers. This means that you can't necessarily control the outcome. If you have a difficult, or incompetent junior lawyer in your team, you are responsible for getting that lawyer to perform good work and/or covering for their failings.

This can be vastly more stressful then simply doing your own job. Equally you may be responsible for liaising with and advising the client at crucial moments. Your calls could determine the success or failure of the legal matter you are working on. If you are a very junior lawyer, you can be comforted by the thought that your work will be reviewed by others and if it was a matter of success or failure, it wouldn't have been left to a lawyer with six months experience. By the time you have been around 5 years, you may be making the crucial calls, drafting the crucial documents and reviewing the work of the junior lawyers to make sure that their inexperience does not destroy what you are achieving. It can be as stressful as hell, but hey, that's why they charge you out at the big bucks.

Chapter 7 - How to get out of a BigLaw firm

You may be a great junior lawyer and decide that you are destined for partnership. You're in for the long haul. For the rest of you, you've probably noticed that the number of associates who make partner at your firm is less than 10 per cent of your intake. That means that there will be an awful lot of people who leave the law firm within the first five years, and that will probably include you.

Don't worry. The world of legal practice is much richer and more interesting than you realize as a junior lawyer sitting in a BigLaw office. You have a good law degree and experience at a well-regarded law firm which means that the options are out there, if you want to pursue them.

This chapter isn't about encouraging people to leave their BigLaw jobs. BigLaw jobs are secure, well-paid, well-supported and offer a clear career path. If you have law school debts or are supporting a family you may not be in a position to take a risk and leave them. However there are plenty of people who:

- hate their BigLaw jobs;
- are made physically sick or mentally ill by their BigLaw Jobs;
- should otherwise not be working at BigLaw; or
- have richer and more interesting opportunities elsewhere;

only they have the BigLaw blinkers on and don't have the guts or awareness of what else is out there and leave for a more satisfying role. Don't be one of those people. Know the options and know if you should get out, when you should get out and where you should get out to.

This chapter should be read as a general guide. The decision to leave a BigLaw firm depends so much on the individual; how they are enjoying BigLaw, what they would rather do, what the employment situation is like elsewhere, how important money is etc. Take this as a guide and talk to people to work out what you should do.

Should you get out?

There are two situations where you should unthinkingly leave your firm, even if only for a period of time. They are:

- If you are doing yourself serious physical or mental harm by staying there and there is no obvious prospect of improvement; or
- If you are being physically, sexually or emotionally abused by a member of the firm (especially a partner) and the firm is doing nothing about it.

This shouldn't even be a question but it is amazing how often people stick with a firm in the above circumstances. If you have suffered a physical collapse from overwork, are suffering from regular panic attacks, or are contemplating suicide, get serious help and leave the place that is causing you trouble. Life is too short to spend 12 or more hours a day in an environment that is your personal hell. No law firm or client is worth it.

Once you have had the collapse, get professional help (it is even better if the firm pays for it). However, unless you have a very good explanation for what caused your collapse, at the minimum, don't return to the same team. Your partner may be understanding about what caused the collapse, and vow to do a better job in the future, but if it was caused by multiple 18 hour days, and their practice regularly requires lawyers to pull 18 hour days, then all his/her good intentions won't prevent a second, and potentially more serious issue. Equally, they may offer you the opportunity to work part time, but again if s/he is in a practice that regularly requires all hands on deck, all part time will mean is that you're working crazy hours to get deals done and being paid half of what others make.

If you can't bear to leave the firm, then try and switch jobs. Move to a different partner with a more laid-back practice, or move to a job within the firm with regular hours (a lot of the practice support lawyers have this). Don't delude yourself into believing that you can go back to your old job as if nothing has happened – you are risking your health to do so. Talk to your friends. If they say you're crazy to do what you do, then you probably are.

Equally, if you are in a situation where a partner or other employee has hit you, or is sexually harassing you or is otherwise abusing you (and the firm does not sack them) get the hell out. What I'm talking about isn't the partner yelling at you or being very critical of your work (you're in the real world now) but physical abuse, sexual harassment or sustained and unwarranted abuse directed at humiliating you. At the minimum, report the issue to HR and the other partners and take a leave of absence. During that time, work out what other options there are for you and what it would take for you to return to the firm and feel comfortable. If you are not satisfied with the outcome of the process then leave the firm. It's not cowardly to do so, but smart. Life is too short to share an office with an abuser. Even if you are transferred to a different team, remember that you might have to share a lift with him/her, or work on a large matter together, or sit on a firm committee together. If you can handle that, then that's fine but again there are plenty of other opportunities for junior lawyers out there that don't involve abuse or being in the presence of your tormentor.

Other than the above two situations, the decision to get out is much harder. Below I break down the good reasons to get out and the no-so-good reasons to get out:

Good reasons to get out

There are better opportunities elsewhere

If you have done your research and you know that another employment option offers you more interesting work/better pay or conditions/better prospects for advancement, then by all means take that job. You owe no loyalty to the firm and you should take the new job.

One caveat to this: If you are working with a good partner you respect at your firm, be careful about giving it up to work at another BigLaw firm, even if it is offering better pay. The reason for this is that good partners retain staff, while bad partners are constantly recruiting. If you do lateral the odds on you ending up with a bad partner are higher than you think, so do your homework in your position before you decide to take the pay increase.

I could get a job in London/New York/Vancouver/Sydney/Singapore etc.

Living in another country or in a big interesting city is a great experience. You'll learn a lot about yourself, make new friends, have fabulous new experiences and have opportunities to travel that you never would otherwise. It won't slow your career progression, and to the extent it does, the experience of living in another city, when you are young and reasonably unencumbered is worth it.

So if you are working in BigLaw in Houston and a job comes up in BigLaw in London, take it. Sure the hours will be just as long, and it won't be fun leaving your friends, but the opportunities to live in London and travel in Europe will make it worth it. Furthermore, you'll see how another firm in another English-speaking country does BigLaw and the experience there will make you a more well-rounded lawyer. Finally if you do return to Houston you can talk to firms about all your great London contacts and how if they need a lawyer in Houston they will of course call you at whatever firm you end up at. This never hurts a partnership application.

I don't want to work in BigLaw

This is a really good reason to get out. If you've decided that BigLaw isn't the place for you then there is no point spending more time in BigLaw, especially if you have hit the two-year mark. However there are two caveats to the above point. They are

- unless you really can't stand BigLaw, don't leave a job until you have a job to go to. You are always a more attractive candidate as an employee or a person studying, then you are as an unemployed person;

- if you do know where you want to go, check to see if there are jobs available at your level of experience. A lot of people leave BigLaw firms for smaller, boutique law firms. However these law firms don't run graduate programs and don't recruit anyone with less than 2-3 years' experience. If you only have one year's experience and a recruiter has told you that they can get you a much better job if you can stick it out for a year, then you might want to stick it out.

I want to work in a particular area of law and I can't get there in this firm.

You may have dreamed all your life of working in IP litigation. Unfortunately your firm has 50 partners, only one of whom does IP Litigation, and they've got a junior s/he loves. You're in the wrong place and you should start looking for a new firm that will give you the opportunities you want.

However before you move, are you really certain it is the opportunity you want? Too many lawyers dream of working in IP Litigation/White Collar Defense/Civil Rights/name a glamorous area of law and then when they get there, they find out that it isn't what they wished for. Do your research and don't pick an area of law to practice based on what you thought was fun in law school. Reality is very different to law school.

Not so good reasons to get out

I don't like the partner/team I'm working with (and you are on rotation).

As a junior lawyer, you become more employable the more experience you get. If you are 1 month in, and you don't like your partner, be wary about jumping ship at this stage. Not only are you only stuck with that partner for the rotation period, it is unlikely that any other significant firm is going to pick up a graduate lawyer who walked out of a law firm and whose practical legal experience is measured in weeks. If you are doing yourself mental or physical harm being there, or the partner is being abusive, of course you should get out but otherwise try and stick it out until the end of the rotation.

If you are now out of rotation, reasonably employable and (for example) your partner retires and you are forced to move to a new and bad partner, you should absolutely consider jumping to another partner or another jobs.

I don't like the clients we work for

As lawyers, you have to represent your client's interests regardless of your own personal views of their behavior. If you work for BigLaw that means representing cigarette companies, mining companies, companies that outsource jobs, rich individuals behaving unethically and other people you criticized at college and university.

While it is understandable that you might question your life choices after another day defending a cigarette company, you should have realized this at the time you signed up to work for your BigLaw firm. In the real world, unless you do public interest law (and acting for the homeless is no picnic either) you will have clients you have issues with. There is no point moving to another BigLaw firm (they will have the same client base as yours), and small law firms are often no panacea (Criminals don't make the most sympathetic clients, and there are plenty of dubious small businesses who are represented by small law firms). Finally if you are determined to use your legal skills for good, then the first task is to develop your legal skills. If the best place to develop those legal skills is in your BigLaw firm, then you are doing yourself a disservice by leaving early.

If you genuinely have a legitimate emotional reaction or a personal conflict with the work you are personally doing (for example your team is defending a cigarette company, and you have had family members that have died from smoking), then talk to your partner about the issue. It might be possible to remove you from the matter and replace you with someone else (all junior lawyers are replaceable). If you are a good junior lawyer and have a decent partner then accommodations can and will be made, but don't play this card more than once: You don't want to be known as the unreliable bleeding-heart lawyer.

Our firm's main competitor is offering 10K more

There is nothing wrong with leaving a firm to take more money at a rival firm. If you are doing the same work in similar conditions, why not go for the more higher-paying firm. However before making the jump consider the following issues:

- Does the other firm consistently pay better than our firm or is it a one-off? The benefit of jumping is pretty minimal if by next year you are making the same as you would have made at your existing firm.
- As you are now aware that the most important element in your experience is your partner. Before you make the jump, consider who would you be working with? Why is he/she recruiting externally? Could it be that nobody in the firm wants to work with him/her?
- Do you know people at the firm? Can you make a social network in the new firm? A social network within a firm is a very valuable thing. You learn which partners are good and not good to work for. You know when to apply for promotion, and what to do in particular circumstances and dealing with particular senior people in the firm. If you have friends who are slightly ahead of you in the firm, they may support your candidacy for partnership when it comes around. As the minimum they will be good drinking buddies at social events. If you lateral in to a new law firm you won't have that law graduate/summer associate network which may hurt your progress in the firm.

In short, unless you are in a bad situation at your firm, don't jump to a similar firm for a short term gain. Look at which firm is best for your long term plans.

Our firm is in crisis

Firms suffer scandals all the time. Partners jump ship all the time. The mere fact that 10 out of the 100 partners in your team have jumped ship in the past year isn't a good reason to leave a law firm. What looks like a firm in crisis from inside the firm can look very different from outside the firm. What may be the reality is that your firm is left with 90 solid partners, with 90 solid practices, and loyal institutional clients. That is not a firm that is going under soon. Equally, if your firm has been hit by a recession and is laying off staff, that doesn't necessarily mean you should leave – other firms will be going through the same pressures and you're safer at a firm where you have a reputation and contacts than at a new firm.

At the same time BigLaw firms do go into bankruptcy. Branch offices of BigLaw firms do close, so be more careful if you are working in a poorly performing, recently established branch office or one that just lost its rainmaker. In those times individual partners may jump ship and try and take their team with them. Talk to your partner about that possibility. Just remember that most firms in crisis end up fine, and you should only really worry if your firm is in a death spiral, with every partner talking about leaving.

I'm sick and tired of due diligence/discovery/amending documents to put in changes that other people have made

This is a complex question: Do you hate all of BigLaw work, or simply the work you are asked to do as a junior lawyer. Because it does get better. Fourth year associates generally don't do due diligence or discovery or other brain deadening work, they do more relevant things, and the quality of work does increase the more senior you get.

What this means is that you need to look at the lawyers 2-4 years more senior than you in the firm. If you can't imagine you doing the work that they do and even being moderately satisfied as a lawyer and human being then get out when it suits you. If you can imagine doing the work that they do, try and stick it out a bit longer. Maybe take a holiday to refresh yourself, or try and get some more interesting work from your partner or another partner. Working in BigLaw is, compared to most jobs, extremely secure and well-paid so don't throw away your career for short term reasons.

When you should get out

This section should not be read as a bible because it depends on

- what you want to do;
- what the condition of the local market is. Different firms in different markets recruit lawyers at different levels of experience. For example generally the path to partnership is shorter in a US firm than an equivalent UK firm, which affects when you want to transfer as part of a plan to become a partner. Equally there is no point in leaving your firm if there are no jobs in your market to go to; and
- What your economic situation is. The reality is that many (though not all) of the options for lawyers wishing to leave BigLaw will pay less. If you have student loans or significant debts, that is obviously a relevant consideration about when to leave your high-paying job for a more satisfying but lower paying job.

If you are planning to get out, talk to recruiters, talk to people who have left the firm and moved into the area that you want to go to about what level of experience they are looking for and the opportunities available. This will help you gauge whether you should get out now for your new opportunity or if you should wait at the law firm. Below I have set out what options are available depending when you decide to leave. Again these vary due to market conditions.

6 months law firm experience

Unless you have significant personal issues, you really should be able to survive 6 months in a law firm. If you decide to leave after 6 months, your options are really limited to non-law firm jobs. Leave after six months if you:

- Realize that the law is a mistake and you want to try teaching/writing/travelling etc.
- Realize that you don't want to be a lawyer, but want to work in a law-adjacent area, such as in the criminal justice system, the public service, business or any other option where a law degree itself is valuable but experience as a lawyer is not a necessity. If you have decided that you want to become a civil servant, then spending an extra 2 years doing M&A is not going to help you become a civil servant.

Don't leave after 6 months if you want to stay a lawyer. BigLaw firms have filled up their graduate position roles and aren't likely to have any spare slots for someone who left their firm after 6 months. SmallLaw firms won't take anyone with less than 2 years' experience. The same is the case for in-house roles. Also unless you have a very good reason, leaving a firm after 6 months as a graduate lawyer looks terrible on your resume/CV.

2 years law firm experience.

At this level you can start moving to other lawyer jobs in other law firms. If you work in a transferrable, and highly valued area (deals, tax advisory) you can move to other large law firms, including large law firms internationally. At this point you should be vaguely competent at the basics of being a lawyer and are attractive to firms that need competent warm bodies to put in their team to work on large transactions or litigations. Equally, from this point forward specialist boutique firms that don't want to train graduate lawyers start recruiting lawyers from BigLaw. If you have always wanted to do international trade law at a specialist firm, now is the time to start looking at your options.

5 years law firm experience

All of the above roles plus in-house roles. Working in-house requires a very specific set of skills. They include the ability to make legal calls without supervision, deal directly with non-legal clients (business units), manage external lawyers, and stick to budgets. With a few exceptions, there are very few lawyers of under 5 years' experience who have all these skills and hence in-house roles are usually targeted at those with greater than 5 years' experience.

Equally if you want to stay in BigLaw, but are conscious of your partnership prospects, you should start considering whether you are likely to make partner at your current firm, or whether you should move firms to improve your odds.

Finally, if you (or you and a few friends) want to hang out your own shingle, now is probably the time to do so. By this stage you are probably a fairly competent junior lawyer, know how to deal with clients, and have sufficient financial resources to start your own firm. It's not an easy job but if it's your dream now is as good a time as any to make that jump.

8-12 years law firm experience

All of the above plus partner roles. Different markets have different timetables as to when someone makes partner, but it is as this stage of your career you should seriously consider moving if you want to be a partner and your path is blocked. The decision as to where and when to move has too many factors to fairly consider here.

Where you should go to

I don't want this chapter to sound like a law school careers office. Of course you can do anything with a law degree and BigLaw experience is highly valued in many markets. People leave BigLaw to do extraordinary things (Barack Obama) as well as the most utterly ordinary things. However junior lawyers commonly leave their BigLaw job for the following places:

Another BigLaw job

This is the easiest transfer of them all. You know what you are getting out of. You know what you are getting into. You've presumably got a good reason to transfer. You can do this as early as the 2 year mark and it is something that reasonably easy to arrange directly or through a legal recruiter.

Another BigLaw job in a different location

There are many reasons why you would want to do a similar job in a different location. You might want to move to a big city, a different country or a practice that more suits your interests. You may have a partner who has to move for his/her job and you are following them. All good reasons to move, however you there are some things you should bear in mind.

Some skill-sets are more easily transferable than others. Deals work can be done anywhere and if you are a good M&A lawyer, the world is your oyster. On the other hand if your skills are jurisdiction specific (advisory based on a particular state or national law, litigation relying on your knowledge of local civil procedure) then interstate and international transfers are more problematic. If you are a tax advisory lawyer in Toronto, your detailed knowledge of the Income Tax Act is probably less useful in Hong Kong than it would be in Vancouver. This doesn't mean that your skills at reviewing and analyzing taxation legislation wouldn't be useful in a Hong Kong role, but you may need to be more careful selling yourself and may have to take a step back in seniority (i.e. Hong Kong law firms may have trouble selling you as a senior tax expert but may be able to sell you as a junior tax expert).

Equally, it is worthwhile checking the admission requirements and the practical necessity for being admitted. Again, if you are an M&A

lawyer, you can work for some time in an interstate or foreign jurisdiction without being admitted, while lawyers who have to appear in court, as well as people at partnership level, need to get admitted quickly.

You may also want to consider whether this move is a temporary or permanent move. If you have moved to London for a few years to travel before moving back home, you perhaps don't need to worry as much about building a client base and reputation there as if you were moving to Houston because your spouse's family is from there.

Finally, as similar as BigLaw firms are internationally, there will still be an initial culture clash. You may struggle with the different hours, different ways that lawyers and staff relate to each other, different levels of formality and different ways the firm is managed (the use of legal technology varies enormously between countries as well as firms). Ideally talk to people from your part of the world who have moved jurisdictions and who understand the transition. A couple of broad cultural issues to beware of:

- If you are moving from the US (or Canada, or Australia) to the UK, you will face the stereotype that you are loud, talkative and obnoxious. When you get to the UK, at least initially tone your behavior down. Once you are established as a professional and respected in the team, you can then behave 'normally'.
- There are two stereotypes about US BigLaw lawyers that drive lawyers from the rest of the world nuts.
  o that they have never-ending phone calls; and
  o that they draft absurdly long, overly formal contracts (using 5 words when one will do).

  If you are moving to the US from the UK, Canada or Australia, you'll just have to grin and bear it, and fight for plain English drafting, one contract at a time. If you are moving from the US, try and adapt to the local customs regarding phone calls and take a few seminars on plain English drafting (i.e. don't use aforementioned, forgoing or include more than one sub-clause per paragraph).

- There are a couple of unique aspects of US law firms that are different from non-US law firms and lawyers making the move one way or another can get tripped up on them:
  - o In US Law firms it is much more accepted to run your personal life through your office; i.e. get your secretary to book flights and manage loyalty programs, have mail delivered to your office. At the same time, you are expected to buy your secretary a large and expensive Christmas gift!
  - o US BigLaw firms generally have much larger bonuses paid to all legal staff members at the end of the year. However they generally (although not universally) have higher billable hour targets.
  - o US BigLaw firms generally have a faster progression to partnership, but are more aggressive in weeding out 10th year associates who don't progress to partner. Outside the US, it is not uncommon to see a senior associate who has been with the same BigLaw Firm for 15 years. Outside the few who transition to of counsel roles, this is very rare in the US.

SmallLaw and Boutique law

This is discussed more in the small law section but when considering a transfer consider the difference between a small general law firm (SmallLaw) and a boutique specialist law firm, and the pluses and minuses of each move. A further important consideration is that in a BigLaw firm, if you don't 'fit' in a team you can transfer to another team reasonably easily. This doesn't exist in SmallLaw so they will analyze fit very closely, as should you.

Equally, in SmallLaw you will be doing a wider variety of work, with more direct client contact and with fewer resources than you are used to in BigLaw. Make sure you are comfortable with the change and persuade your future employers about how comfortable you are with this change.

Legal Counsel roles

The big escape route. 80% of the prestige, 70% of the pay, 50% of the hours!

I just made that up. The role of legal counsel has changed and expanded enormously and varies tremendously between businesses. Many larger corporations have extensive legal departments that operate as mini-law firms, and there are certainly legal counsel who work BigLaw hours for BigLaw pay.

Nevertheless there are plenty of opportunities in the legal counsel space for lawyers who wish to continue practicing law, but do so freed from the constraints of BigLaw. In general there are several advantages to practicing in this area including:

- No billable hours requirement;
- If the work gets too busy, then subject to your budget, you can outsource it to an external law firm (pay the external lawyers to work on the weekend, while you enjoy yourself);
- The opportunity to work continuously for one client and really understand its business, what drives the business and what the business is looking for in legal advice and support.

Of course there are several disadvantages including:

- You have to jump from being a specialist to a generalist. You may have spent the last 5 years in BigLaw doing M&A deals, but the first thing across your desk may be a property dispute for your corporation; Or being asked to approve an ad; or being asked to draft a contract (without a precedent). You will do this with few precedents, external search resources or general support. Get comfortable begging colleagues for precedents.

- It becomes harder to stay on the cutting edge of a particular area of law. Most counsel are to some degree generalists, and even counsel from large corporations cover more areas of the law then their counterparts at law firms. Furthermore, there are generally fewer CLEs and formal training opportunities while practicing as a legal counsel.

- There is a perception (but one that may be changing) that once you become a legal counsel, you can't jump back into a law firm, other than at a very senior level (i.e. if you bring the company back as a client, a firm will make you partner).

- There is a loss of status. Lawyers are the reason a law firm exists. Firms hold parties to celebrate them. Support services exist to serve them. Promotional material is printed to praise them. In-house counsel are either simply 'Legal', the 'Sales Prevention Unit' or a 'cost-center' to be cut in times of crisis. You're not the main game in the company, rather the road block between the people who generate the profit and the profit (you also save these people when they do stupid things, but nobody ever remembers that). A well run corporation will ensure the right level of support and respect to legal counsel but not all firms are this well run.

Like all areas of law, being a legal counsel has its ups and downs and varies greatly depending on the size and sophistication of the company you work for. However in order to get these roles it helps to have around 5 years' experience so that you are comfortable regularly making legal calls yourself. Equally, companies are looking for lawyers with very good people skills, rather than necessarily pure technical skills. You may be the greatest contract drafter of all time, but if you can't clearly talk to the business, ask the right questions, take instructions correctly and explain politely to the business person that the term can't be included in the contract because it is illegal, then you have no place in a legal counsel role. Equally, if you can't give practical advice, including advice where you are able to quantify the legal risk, you have no place as a legal counsel. Many transactions include some legal risk and it is up to the decision-maker to determine if the risk should torpedo the transaction. S/he won't appreciate you if you simply say no to every transaction without identifying the risk, quantifying it, outlining the possible outcomes if the transaction goes ahead and the best strategies for minimizing that risk. In short you need to be a real lawyer who provides solutions, not a billing and drafting machine.

Legal Industry roles – Recruiter, Researcher, Professional support, Legal Consultant

An often overlooked career path for junior lawyers is other legal industry support roles, which are often stacked with BigLaw refugees. A large percentage of legal recruiters are ex-lawyers, which isn't surprising since they come to the recruiting industry with an in-built client base. Equally a surprising number of professional support people at the firm have a legal background. Obviously, the precedents people and the legal researchers have a legal background, but if you look around the legal technology space, there are a number of ex-lawyers who decided to use their skills to develop technology to make the life of lawyers easier (or just make them do more work in the same number of hours). Equally many of the professional managers and legal consultants employed by law firms to manage staff, build client relationships and improve professional development are ex-lawyers.

If you want to stop practicing law, but don't want to put your experience in BigLaw to waste, it may be possible to leverage your skills and contacts into one of these roles. It is worthwhile talking to people in these roles about how they moved into these roles and your interest in the area as new roles within law firms in the professional support area are often unadvertised and can be filled with an ex-lawyer. In particular firms are keen to employ ex-lawyers in the marketing and client relationship space as they can understand the pressures of practicing law while discussing a matter with the client and passing on feedback to the legal team, so if that is your interest you will be pushing at an open door.

Legal Academic roles

There aren't too many of these roles out there but they do attract a few people who leave BigLaw. There are three types of people who end up moving from law firm practice to academia:

a) The young star. You probably finished number one in your class, wrote a thesis that re-defined constitutional law and had a stint as a clerk in the Supreme Court. After two years of 'slumming it' in the top law firm in the city, you are happy enough to devote your brain to the law and not to discovery.

b) The older star. You were the leading partner in your field, with a number of successful cases under your belt, but you are interested in a change of scenery. A professorship is a nasty pay cut but there are things more important than the money.

c) The specialist grinder: You were a good student at law school and work at a good law firm but would like to move to an academic career and share what little you know with the students.

If you are category c and wish to move into a legal academic role there are three things that you should start doing immediately:

a) Teaching: if your local law school is interested in getting local practitioners to take tutorials, run seminars or run summer courses, apply for these roles. It gets you a foot in the door and helps you know if the academic life is for you. If you have been tutoring or running seminars with an academic and they like you, he/she'll be a great support if you apply for a more permanent job. The challenge is getting sufficient time off work to take this role (you need a supportive partner). Even if you aren't able to teach, offer to take a guest seminar where you can share your legal knowledge just to get your foot in the door.

b) Write. Law firm journals are desperate for content, It may be hard to find the time but if you can point to a couple of existing law journal articles, that can only help your prospects of moving into a legal academic role. You don't even need to have an idea; a good law firm journal editor may have any number of ideas that s/he is waiting for someone to write on. Pick your journal, talk to the editor and see how you can assist. Equally if you co-write an article with someone in the faculty, that will help your prospects for any roles that arise.

c) Start studying for a PhD. Unless you are the older star, a doctorate is almost an entry requirement into academia, so time to think about that thesis topic.

Non-legal roles but ones in which a law degree isn't a hindrance – civil servant, business

Retrain entirely for a different profession.

There is not much to say about these two options. Just because you have a law degree doesn't mean you have to be a lawyer. Remember a law degree is a sunk cost and staying in a profession that doesn't suit you will not make you happy. There are plenty of interesting, challenging jobs out there for ex-lawyers – you just need to find them and make them happen.

How you should get out

The first piece of advice is never leave a job unless you have a new one lined up. You are always much more employable when you are in an existing job. The only exceptions are if you have to leave the firm for your sake, or you are prepared to take a significant period of time off (say 6 months) to travel the world, volunteer or find yourself.

The next piece of advice is never leave your firm on bad terms. The world of law is small, and with the advent of the internet, even smaller. Don't dump on your old firm, attack a partner, or write an 'epic' departure memo. You never know when you will see these people again, or will meet people who have read your 'epic' memo (and were not amused by it) on Legal Cheek or Above the Law.

Talk to your friends/networks. This is why you spent time hanging out with the other lawyers at your firm at Friday drinks, maintaining LinkedIn networks and staying in touch with law school friends on Facebook. Your friends can advise you about where to go, and what a particular employer is looking for. They may be aware of jobs that don't even exist. Finally a lot of firms offer bonuses to existing employees if they can bring in new, qualified staff (saving them the costs of a recruiter). If you want to go to a new firm, and have a friend there, why not get him/her to vouch for you. You get a new job, they get a nice bonus, and you get a free meal from said friend (and if they doesn't buy you a free meal after getting the referral bonus, that person really shouldn't be your friend).

Finally recruiters; the real estate agents of the profession. They don't have the greatest of reputations but, if you are moving in house or between law firms they do perform a necessary role, and they do it (for you) for free. More importantly they may be aware of opportunities in the market that you weren't aware of and can benchmark your salary expectations. The good ones (and there are good ones out there) will even try and match you to a role that you fit into (it does no good to a recruiter's reputation if they repeatedly shoe-horn bad fits into law firms; a law firm is going to be quite wary of anybody the recruiter puts forward next time). My advice is (again) talk to friends to see if they can recommend a recruiter, and if not find 2-3 specialist ones (i.e. don't go to a recruiter who specializes in international transfers if you are planning on moving in-house) and meet with them to decide which one works best. Also don't, at least initially, sign on with 2-3 recruiters. It will annoy the recruiters and law firms, and since the recruiter is doing a job for you, there is no need to make their job harder. At the same time, if after a month or two you are getting no-where, by all means break up with your recruiter and move on. A new recruiter may be able to find opportunities that the previous ones missed.

Chapter 8 – The wonderful world of SmallLaw

The vast majority of this book has dealt with issues arising out of the practice of law in large, sophisticated law firms, with large sophisticated clients. The reason for this is that many junior lawyers cut their teeth in large law firms and then strike-out on their own or join small law firms that provide services to the community. However there are plenty of junior lawyers who leave law school and start work for a small practice and this section of the book is for them.

So what is SmallLaw? Is it just small firms? Not necessarily; there are plenty of highly sophisticated boutique firms specializing in an area of law that have corporate clients. Is it just single-partner firms? Again not necessarily.

The key distinction between SmallLaw and BigLaw is in the clients. BigLaw firms usually deal with corporations or high-net-worth individuals. They are normally instructed by legal counsel, who are lawyers themselves and thus understand the technical nature of legal advice. The partners and teams specialize exclusively in one area of law and tend to be located in large fancy CBD office blocks. SmallLaw firms tend to deal with the legal problems of individuals and small businesses. They are rarely instructed by counsel and are usually instructed by the individual themselves, or the owner/manager of the business. While they may attempt to market themselves as specialists in a particular areas, they generally handle a wide variety of their client's needs. They locate themselves where the clients are; in the CBD, suburbs or small towns; in fancy office buildings, business parks or in suburban high streets/strip malls. They don't have to be tiny – indeed a 5 partner, 10 lawyer firm can be a SmallLaw firm. They provide access to the law to the average person/business owner, and perform a vital role in our legal system.

In this chapter I will talk about the surprising ways in which SmallLaw and BigLaw are the same, and the many ways in which they differ.

Ways SmallLaw and Big Law are the same

Complexity of disputes and advices

One of the great misconceptions of BigLaw is that BigLaw Lawyers do the tough, complex cases, while small-law cases and advices are simple. That is utterly untrue. While some SmallLaw disputes are minor criminal matters, it is amazing how complex legal issues can be in commercial matters handled by SmallLaw firms. In particular, contract disputes often raise complex interpretation issues, issues of equity, jurisdictional issues and the like. Moreover, instead of these issues being grappled with by some of the top legal minds that populate the superior courts, they are being grappled with by an underpaid public servant at a small town courthouse which puts extra pressure on the lawyers to explain the legal principles in a clear, logical and simply way. Many tort cases involve a plaintiff being represented by SmallLaw and the defendant being represented by BigLaw. Both sides are grappling with the same complex legal issues. Sometimes seemingly simple legal questions from small businesses can lead you down a legal rabbit-hole. Finally, because of the breadth of clients of SmallLaw, SmallLaw firms deal with areas of law that BigLaw don't touch, including crime, family, conveyancing, estate and the like. A junior lawyer in a BigLaw firm will almost never deal with a complex dispute involving wills, estate planning and the conveyancing of property, while a junior lawyer in SmallLaw may well deal with all these areas in his/her first two years.

Working hours (potentially)

This is one of the great myths of SmallLaw; that you work 9-5. Unlike in BigLaw where you can be pretty confident that you will work long hours, in SmallLaw you may work 9-5, but you may just as easily work 8-midnight. Plenty of SmallLaw firms have lots of work and a very small number of lawyers to do it. Equally, there are layers of support in BigLaw that aren't there in small-law. As bad as life in BigLaw is, just remember that there are Small-Law lawyers who are manually inputting changes into a complex document at 1am. At that hour there is no secretarial support, no late meals, no IT support and the photocopier has almost certainly broken down.

SmallLaw does provide lawyers with the opportunity to work better business hours; the overheads are lower, the salaries are lower and the clients are (sometimes) less demanding. Many SmallLaw lawyers do work 9-5, especially those who don't work in large cities. However, law is a complex and difficult business, regardless of where you work and as a junior lawyer, you may well be the one working BigLaw hours on a SmallLaw salary.

Needing to satisfy a partner

Like BigLaw, your job as a junior lawyer is do the work your partner gives you, do it well and make him or her look good. Doing a good job builds the partner's confidence in you and soon you will get more interesting and more substantive work. Ultimately your aim is to develop your skills and reputation within the firm and try and build the most interesting, satisfying and successful career. The only way to get there as a junior lawyer, is doing what the partner wants, when the partner wants, in the manner in which the partner wants, regardless of the size of the law firm.

The vital importance of not being a dick

One of the reasons junior lawyers get fired from BigLaw is for being a dick. Not being a dick is even more important in SmallLaw. If you are a technically brilliant workaholic in BigLaw you can survive being a dick (they'll put you in your own office and leave you there until you make counsel), but if you are a dick in SmallLaw, you have no chance of survival. The office is too small, you see clients too often and there is too much gossiping and interpersonal conflict for a junior lawyer who is difficult to work with, temperamental or treats people badly, to survive. Remember in a BigLaw firm, a partner has to answer to HR and management before firing an associate. In SmallLaw, once one or two partners decide you are not worth it, you better pack your bags and start looking for a new job or a new career.

Ways SmallLaw and BigLaw are different

Less homogenous

SmallLaw firms are vastly less homogenous than BigLaw firms. BigLaw firms, even those in different countries, have the same basic elements; a partner-lawyer relationship, and obsession with billing, sophisticated corporate clients, long hours, regular social events, layers of bureaucracy, nice offices and (generally) excellent technology and support.

SmallLaw firms can vary enormously based on the people who work there and the leadership of the firm. Some of them are dedicated to working limited hours; some of them are very hard-working. Some of them specialize in certain areas of the law; some of them take any client. Some of them are happy, collegial places to work; some of them are nightmares. Some of them have excellent technology and due to their size, can be more nimble than BigLaw firms in being flexible and mobile; while others have barely functional technology. Simply, there is a massive variation between firms and any strategy to succeed in a small firm or move SmallLaw firms has to take into account the individual nature of the firm. Moreover, the atmosphere of a firm is created by its people; and it might only take one or two staffing changes at a SmallLaw firm to change the culture of the firm significantly, for good or bad; such that the SmallLaw firm that you started with is not the one you are working for two years later.

Complexity of transactions

While litigation and advisory work in SmallLaw firms can be just as legally complex as in BigLaw, the transactions are almost always less complex. While there are legal complexities in the purchase of small allotments of property, the sale of a medium sized business, or the financing of a business expansion, the factual and legal complexity cannot be compared to the sale of a large, public company, which may involve multiple different financing parties, different levels of security, massive due diligence to ensure that the buyer is not incurring a risk in buying the company and a general level of factual complexity that is well and truly beyond what exists in SmallLaw. In short, if you want to do the most complex of deals, you are really limited to working in BigLaw, or as in house counsel to a company that regularly participates in deals. Furthermore, in most SmallLaw firms the junior lawyer will be doing a lot of wills and estates work, which in most cases is fairly simple.

On the other hand, if you want regular transactions that require a good sense of detail, general savvy but do not require 100 lawyers at 5 different firms working 90 hour weeks to pull off, perhaps SmallLaw is for you.

Different billing practices

Billing at BigLaw is very simple. Bill everything and let the partner write it off. Billing at SmallLaw is much more complex and depends greatly on the individual firm. Some firms do operate on the traditional 'Bill everything and let the partner write it off' but for most it is more complex than that. If you are one of three lawyers in an office, everyone can see how hard you are working, so the benefit of billables as a measure of performance is overstated. Secondly as a SmallLaw lawyer, even one that is very junior you will either:

- o be responsible for finalizing bills to clients; and/or
- o be fully aware of what the client can or cannot pay and what the firm can or cannot bill.

This means that your firm may have a policy of 'record only what you can bill to the client'. More importantly, you have to be much more disciplined about how you spend your time on a client's matter. If the client only has limited funds, you aren't assisting the firm in going on a 2 day frolic to consider a potential constitutional issue, or spending money on online legal research that isn't necessary. Your work has to be very strictly limited to what you think you can bill the client for and then you record that time. You may need to exercise that judgment call; not leave it to your partner.

Fewer resources (precedents, research, IT support)

You may be working equally long hours. You may be doing equally complex work at an earlier stage in your career. You may be going to court against an associate from a much larger firm and you will be doing all this with vastly fewer resources than you would at BigLaw.

Most BigLaw firms have well-stocked libraries with relevant textbooks and casebooks. They have access to online resources and may well have that access on an 'unlimited search' basis meaning that you can search what you what, when you want. They have detailed stacks of precedents, lots of previous work stored on the central server, 24 hour IT support, 24 hour secretarial and WP support and well-trained librarians to assist.

At SmallLaw you will have little or none of that. In particular your research resources will be limited to a few textbooks, and your online searches will be limited to what is free and what the client is willing to pay for on a search by search basis. Your firm may maintain precedents, but it will be more of the 'Hey do you have a copy of a sale of business agreement for a pharmacy which deals with the regulation in the Act' rather than a searchable database. 24 hour support is a dream.

One of the great benefits of technology in the legal sector is that has closed the gaps between SmallLaw and BigLaw. Legislation is available online, as are many cases and some low cost search tools. It is possible, for a reasonably low price, to buy access to precedents and if all else fails, Google is a great friend of the junior lawyer (but don't rely on everything you read on the Internet).

Generally more flexible

At BigLaw you are part of a big bureaucracy. You will need to accept standardized pay and bonuses, standardized holidays, regular reporting requirements, facetime requirements and billable hour targets. At SmallLaw you are really at the mercy of your boss, and possibly the office administrator. This can be good or bad.

The good is that if you do want a more flexible arrangement with the firm, you may be able to negotiate it. Want to go part time – it doesn't hurt to ask. Want to work one day a week from home - again it can be negotiated. If you have kids and want to work from 6.30am-3pm and your boss is fine with this then go ahead. If the firm is quiet and you want to take time off then you can talk to the boss about it. In short, while I'm not suggesting that you should take advantage of the partners in a SmallLaw firm, it is easier to have them adjust to your needs if you are a good employee and they are good people.

The downside of this is if the firm is old-fashioned and inflexible. You may be at a firm where the partner insists that you be present between 8.30 and 5.30 each day. They may be opposed to any working from home and/or won't allow you to access your work from home. They may institute strict billable hour targets and otherwise oppose all flexibility. They may be so busy that they refuse to grant leave or consider flexible working arrangements because it's all too hard. One of the advantages of BigLaw is that they do have HR people who are aware of modern trends of staff benefits, and partners who are aware of the need to retain staff, so conditions do reflect modern workplace realities. The nature of SmallLaw should allow for more flexibility however there are some idiosyncratic firms that are stuck in the past.

Less time to work on matters – need for value for money

In BigLaw, you are pressed by deadlines, and the need to provide value for money, but otherwise you are not discouraged on spending as much time on a client's matter as necessary. The client may have a budget for a matter that the firm has to comply with, but they also have the resources, and the firm may take the view that a really great outcome is worth the additional expense to be billed to the client.

In SmallLaw, unless the client is particularly well-off, you have a much stricter budget. The client can't afford the Rolls-Royce service you might want to provide in BigLaw, rather you have to do the best you can on a tight budget. In BigLaw you might feel that it is impossible to take a matter to hearing for less than $100,000, but in SmallLaw you'll discover that it is quite possible to run matters for $20,000 if you cut a few corners. You might not like cutting corners and it might hurt the client in the long run but your job is to do the best job for your client at a price they can afford. This means every step in a litigation (for example) is considered on a cost benefit analysis; do we need to get an expert in or will s/he be too expensive for the benefit? Do we want to put in an application for discovery, or can we get by without discovery? Do we want to try and strike out their claim, or will this just delay the matter and cost our client money? All these matters suddenly become legitimate considerations when you are trying a case worth $100,000 instead of $100 million!

Steeper learning curve

The learning curve in SmallLaw is vastly steeper than in BigLaw. SmallLaw doesn't have vast due diligence or discovery projects for their junior lawyers to work on, rather you will slide straight into the practice of law. Within 6 months you may well be meeting clients on your own, providing legal advice, attending settlements, drafting documents, managing your own files and even attending court. If you have a bad boss who doesn't take the time to guide and train you, this will be utterly terrifying, and you will have no doubt committed professional malpractice by then, but (sadly) that's all part of life in SmallLaw.

The downside of this learning curve is that you will be constantly placed in situations beyond your experience level where you will make embarrassing mistakes. The only way to reduce this risk is through good communications with your partner, and good advice from other lawyers in the firm. The upside is, two years in, when you are having lunch with a law school buddy who is at a BigLaw firm (hopefully they are paying) and s/he mentions that in two years s/he's never been to court, met a client, or handled a matter by himself/herself, you can feel like a real lawyer, who actually practices law instead of shuffling papers for 12 hours a day!

In short, if you actually want to appear in court, interact with a client, argue with opposing lawyers and deal with complex and challenging work early in your career (and avoid due diligence, discovery and drafting 100 page contracts), then you should practice in SmallLaw.

Less supervision

In BigLaw you are working on large matters for sophisticated clients. No sophisticated client is likely to put a matter in the hands of a first year associate (the legal counsel, who is probably ex-BigLaw and been a lawyer for 10 years, knows much better). Your work as a junior lawyer will be closely supervised and you will start in the sandpit where you can do the least harm. That isn't the case in SmallLaw.

You may work for a partner who is closely involved in your work but they have a busy practice to run, and may not have time to hold your hand. You will also be acting for non-legal customers. To them you are a real lawyer and certainly know more about the law than anyone else in the room. You will need to make the calls and need to get used to making the calls (and recovering when you make the wrong calls).

More client difficulties

BigLaw clients are demanding, but ultimately rational as to what can and can't be achieved by a law firm. Also you don't have the deal with clients as a junior lawyer; that is the job of the partner.

In SmallLaw you will deal with clients, and it will be difficult, hard and heartbreaking for a number of reasons:

You will have to explain to clients who may be good people, that the law cannot help them in a particular case, and that they may need to accept whatever horrible outcome that they have come to you to escape. My personal hatred is explaining to someone who has voluntarily entered a guarantee that there is no basis (in that particular case) to escape the impact of the guarantee they signed (to guarantee the debt of a family member for example), and that kind, good person is going to go bankrupt. Almost as bad is explaining to a person that they have an issue with the title of their house, meaning that they may not own the property they have put their life savings into.

You may have to explain to clients that they may have a good case, that the law may help them, but that they don't have enough money to run a case and get the outcome they deserve. They may have had money stolen from them by a scammer but you have to tell them that the cost of pursuing the scammer, as well as the difficulty in enforcing any judgment, is such that it is not in their interest to enforce their rights.

You may have to explain to clients who have put their hopes and dreams in you that you have lost or are about to lose a case and that they will lose their house/go bankrupt/lose their job/go back to prison and that all the money they gave to you was a waste. They will often behave with great dignity and kindness during this difficult time and somehow this makes it worse.

You will have to explain law to a non-lawyer; or even worse a non-lawyer who thinks s/he knows something about the law. The non-lawyer may think that the law will assist him/her because it is fair, or it is the right thing to do, or s/he has been screwed over by somebody. You will need to explain the basics of a legal right, a legal cause of action and the importance of admissible evidence. Clients hate (and rightly so) being told that they may have a case but they don't have the documentary evidence to support what they are saying, which means that they shouldn't go through the lottery of the legal system. If they are particularly bad, you will be spending your time, and the client's money, being Dr. No and explaining to the client why every legal theory s/he runs by you is utterly hopeless (and s/he will not appreciate being billed for this time).

You will have to deal with lying, untrustworthy clients. For all the flaws of BigLaw, the clients are generally pretty trustworthy – legal counsel are professionals, who value their reputation and know the importance of telling the truth to a lawyer. SmallLaw clients will tell the most outrageous lies to their lawyers i.e. 'I never read that page… but here is your signature at the bottom of the page… I never read that section… but here are your initials right next to the section… but I was told by the other side to sign it and was told it would never be enforced… But you signed it on a different date to the other side… but I was told by my witness that the other side said it would never be enforced…but your witness didn't have any contact with the other side…' and so on. They will lie about the circumstances of the incident, withhold important pieces of information and even lie about the advice you have given them. Sometimes they don't even know they are lying (most litigation involves witnesses who have reconstructed what occurred in a manner that suits their interests and honestly believe they are telling the truth), but all will swear to an excellent memory of what occurred on that particular day 5 years earlier!

Clients will also lie to you about their net worth, and how much money they have to pay you. Always be wary of a client who is willing to pay 'whatever it takes' to get a result because 'it's the principle'. That client is rarely willing to pay you and can usually be deterred by a request for a nice large sum in trust.

The only way to deal with a lying client is to keep good file notes and call out the client as often as possible. Especially in litigation, it is better for you to keep on calling out the lies in your witness beforehand (i.e. 'you just told me that you were overseas for all of January? Yes. But here's your passport with arrival stamps between 10 and 25 January. Oh I meant all relevant parts of January' and so on…) than them being exposed in cross-examination. File notes are vital; if you lose the case or the deal falls apart the lying client will just as likely go to another lawyer to persuade them to bring a misconduct claim against you. It is great if you can have some nice file notes to persuade that lawyer not to waste his time on that case.

Even if you get clients that aren't lying or untrustworthy, there are clients that are difficult. It may be your job to deal with them. This includes:

- the client who can't pay you and you have to fire. You didn't practice law to threaten your own clients with being sued if they don't pay your bills;
- the client who can't really afford you and therefore quibbles every aspect of your bill 'How can you say you took 1 hour to write a letter to the other side? I can write a letter in 10 mins! You say you spent 24 minutes on a phone call with the opposing lawyer. What did you discuss? How could this take 24 minutes?' You end up spending more time justifying your bill (none of it billable) than working on the matter;
- the client who promises things and then doesn't deliver. Especially clients who promise to provide you with documents supporting their claims in a week, before the

evidence is due, but actually don't provide anything. This equally applies to clients who promise that they have evidence that supports everything they say, only to provide you with an e-mail written by their sister which says that they are an honest person;

- the client who has an over-optimistic view of the law and what will happen with his matter; and operates on the assumption that just because they say something, the judge will believe him/her and find in his favor (regardless of the law applying to his case);
- the client who has an overly pessimistic view of the law and thinks the entire system (including you) is out to get him/her; and/or
- the client who doesn't trust anything you say and demands to speak to your partner about everything.

Experienced lawyers know, through trial and error, how to spot difficult clients, how to get rid of them (tip, give them the local bar association/law society's phone number and tell them to find a better lawyer there), or how to guide them through the litigation process (get everything down on paper, get the money in trust, and add enough money to the estimate to cover all the extra work they are). You, of course have just graduated law school, which aside from a client interview competition, gave you no instructions about how to deal with clients and instead you have to rely on all the savvy you picked up in 12 years of school, 3-7 years of university/college and your summer job at the local McDonalds. On the bright side, unlike your big law buddies, you get to tell the best stories at parties!

More local focus, being part of the community

There is a distinct difference in focus between BigLaw firms and SmallLaw firms. BigLaw firms are heavily national or international in their orientation. If you are in the New York office of a BigLaw firm, your clients could be from anywhere in America or around the world. The lawyers in your team may be from anywhere in America or around the world. You will be working on transactions or litigation involving international companies, or national companies with an international element (i.e. the purchase of an American company with a significant overseas property portfolio). As such your work will have a broad national or global focus.

In SmallLaw, especially SmallLaw in smaller cities and towns, you will have a local focus, with an interest in being part of the community. Your clients will generally be locals, I.e. the other tenants in your building, the people your partner went to school or church with, the ones you met at local small business events, or individuals looking to buy and sell property who know someone who recommended you. The other lawyers you deal with are all likely to be locals, and there is a real focus on being part of the local community, because the more embedded in the life of the local community you are, the more likely you are to get clients. Whether or not you are a person who has developed, or is seeking to develop links in the local community is a factor in whether you should choose to go into SmallLaw, and how successful you are.

Different career opportunities

For better or worse the career opportunities are different depending on whether you start out in a BigLaw or SmallLaw role. In BigLaw you can:

- Easily move to other BigLaw roles;
- Reasonably easily move into SmallLaw roles, providing they are confident that you fit in; or
- Easily move to legal counsel roles with mid and large-sized companies.

However, there is a prejudice against lawyers from SmallLaw firms moving 'up'. Perhaps it is the lack of pedigree, or the lack of polish, or the lack of relevant experience, but it is hard for lawyers who start out in SmallLaw to later transfer into BigLaw. One of the key reasons for that is that much of BigLaw is deals and working in

SmallLaw does not prepare you for the complexity and nature of the deals work done by BigLaw. Equally, time advising Mr. and Mrs. Smith in a tax dispute with the government does not prepare you to join a tax advisory practice.

However, it is easier to make the transition as a litigator; if you can show, for example that you have experience and competence as a litigator acting for plaintiffs in insurance matters; then there is every chance you could be recruited by a BigLaw firm that does insurance defense work.

More mysteriously, there is a prejudice against hiring SmallLaw lawyers for general counsel roles: this is mysterious because general counsel roles often call for generalists, and SmallLaw lawyers are the ultimate generalists. Perhaps there is a degree of 'hiring their own' from general counsels, who tend to recruit people they perceive as talented (i.e. they made it into BigLaw) but want a better lifestyle.

SmallLaw lawyers can easily move into other SmallLaw roles, since a SmallLaw firm can be comfortable that a reasonably experienced SmallLaw lawyer won't struggle with the lesser resources and greater client contact required by SmallLaw. Equally, they can move into roles with small businesses (i.e. if a two person business needs a third person to handle administrative, legal and compliance aspects, the generalist aspect of SmallLaw is very useful). Finally if you are a SmallLaw person desperately hoping to move into BigLaw, my advice (other than move into litigation) is to move into a boutique or mid-tier CBD firm that does the same sort of work as a BigLaw firm. This way you start getting the base of experience in the type of work that a BigLaw firm does, you won't be perceived as a suburban lawyer out of his depth and you will have a resume that looks hirable.

128

Chapter 9 - How to survive SmallLaw

SmallLaw can be the best way to practice law. It can be the worst. What separates good and bad SmallLaw lawyers is whether they can be flexible, creative, personable and keep a sense of humor about the fact that sometimes, you just can't help people.

Lesson 1 - be creative with your resources

You don't have the resources of BigLaw firms. You don't have the textbooks, the researchers, the online access etc. So if you want to do the best job for your client, you have to be creative. This means knowing whether your local law society/bar association has a library with borrowing privileges. Do you have access to a university's law library? What about a library in the city with legal resources? Is there another law firm nearby? Can you make arrangements to share library costs with them? Do your colleagues/friends have law books relevant to the case that you are running?

Equally you are unlikely to have a lovely set of precedents for many of the matters you are running. Do any of your colleagues maintain a personal list of precedents for those types of cases? Do the local courts/litigant assistance bureau maintain some simple precedents to jump off from? Can you beg appropriate precedents from a friend or from a member of whatever junior lawyer listserv you have undoubtedly joined. Once you have been in SmallLaw for a while, you should have your own precedents library from the work you have done. Create a folder of particularly good work you have done and refer back to it when necessary.

You are unlikely to have the same level of IT support, so it's time to get creative. How are you at fixing IT problems? Can you arrange to get access to a third party IT support service in India? You are the young lawyer in the team, see if you can persuade the firm to consider new and innovative ways to run their IT support and/or identify ways to reduce the risk that a firm's entire data isn't destroyed in a single fire. Equally, if your firm does have detailed precedents and they don't work, you are unlikely to have a WP operator available to fix them. This means you need to know how the precedents operate back to front before they break down at 11.30 on a Friday night!

If you are on a large piece of litigation or similar work, against a firm with much larger resources, know your outsourcing providers. There are no shortage of legal service providers who can handle discovery, case research, document management, presentation preparation and provide an online database to keep track of all the relevant documents. If your firm doesn't have the resources, then suggest that the firm use outsourcing providers. Equally, it is possible for a firm to outsource various aspects of its management, including billing, debt recovery, IT support and other services, which can keep a firm lean and mean and able to expand when necessary. Of course using outsourcing providers for large matters depends on the clients having the money to pay for it!

Lesson 2 - constantly focus on costs

BigLaw Lawyers complain about pressure from clients to control costs. They have no idea! They have no idea what it is to practice law when 2 hours work for $500 makes a significant difference to a client. They have no idea what it is like to practice law when a client queries whether it really did take you half an hour to travel to court. They have no idea what it is like to practice law when you have to ring a client every week to get more money in advance, otherwise you stop working on a matter (and restart it after you have missed a bunch of deadlines).

Costs and bills matter in SmallLaw and if you want to succeed you need to know your way around this. Always know your firm policies on billing: what you can bill to a client (and it will vary per client). Always be very clear in writing time narrations: they are being read by a non-lawyer. Always know what your partner's attitude is to writing off your time: for some matters they will be happy to write off if the product is good, and for others they will not agree, and ALWAYS FOCUS ON COSTS!

Be creative in thinking about how you can do work cheaper. Do you have precedents you can use? Can you get the other side to draft the settlement agreement/appear in court for the consent orders? Is there an article you can send to the client in lieu of specific advice? Is there a way you can settle the case for the client that will keep their legal costs low. Obviously, you are in the business of selling your firm's legal services but as a SmallLaw firm, you are hoping to maintain a good reputation and obtain repeat business. The easiest way to keep a client is to do a good job, and bill fairly and reasonably.

Lesson 3 - be good to the client

Clients are really annoying, wherever you practice but as a SmallLaw lawyer you see a lot more of them. Moreover, in most cases the matter is much more important to the SmallLaw client than the BigLaw client. If a BigLaw firm loses a middling contract case, life will go on. If a financing deal falls through, there is usually another way of getting finance. Not so for SmallLaw: that employment discrimination case you are running may be the difference between your client working and being unemployable. That conveyancing you stuffed up may cost your client years' worth of their salary to fix up. That tort claim you lost may mean that your client has to work a second job, or loses his/her business or has to delay his/her retirement. These things really matter.

While it is not necessarily billable; you'll be a better lawyer if you spend a little bit more time with the client then necessary. Take the time to listen to their concerns and reassure them. Take the time to explain the strengths and weaknesses of the case as well as the procedure in the court, and when an outcome is reached. Many non-lawyers have very mistaken assumptions about how the law and how courts work and it is worthwhile exposing those assumptions before clients get angry at you about, for example, a reserved judgement or a delay in enforcing a judgement.

You should also be aware that sometimes the law can't provide the answers. If the law can't help them in a particular situation, can you refer clients to professional counselling, the police, an ombudsman or other agency that can help with their particular issue.

Clients also like to have faith in their lawyer. You may be inexperienced and terrified, but at least show the client you are hard-working and diligent. You don't need to overstate your ability, but don't terrify them with your inexperience either. Show that you understand the case, the laws and the risks that they are running, so they believe in you.

Finally, focus on what they can afford in the context of the matter. If the matter is a $40,000 contract dispute, then don't spend $100,000 on the case (especially in a jurisdiction that doesn't automatically make the loser pay the winner's costs). Talk to the client about the budgetary limits, and what it means you can and can't do. Most clients are fairly understanding, and if the client wants a better case than you think the case needs, that's fine, but they should pay for it. Having the skills to engage with clients will serve you well in your legal career and you should develop them early in SmallLaw.

Lesson 4 - don't be bullied by BigLaw or more experienced lawyers

Soon enough you will have a matter in which you go up against a BigLaw firm or a more experienced lawyer. Don't be bullied by them! Just remember when dealing with BigLaw, if it is a small case, you will be dealing with a junior lawyer, just like you, who is probably less experienced in running litigation than you are. If you are dealing with a more senior lawyer, just remember that you are just as smart as they are, but the only difference is more experience; and you can get around that by being creative and getting lots of advice from more senior lawyers.

Importantly, it is your job to represent the client, and you don't do it by accepting the legal analysis provided to you by the other side: you'd be amazed how often they have missed the point. At the same time, there is no point being needlessly difficult: in most cases the BigLaw firm is trying to resolve the matter at a low cost for their client (there are numerous stories about BigLaw firms extending matters, especially insurance matters, to bankrupt the other side, but more often than not, law firms are under pressure to resolve matters as quickly and low-cost as possible and rarely adopt this strategy; no matter how much you think they are doing that).

Remember, that in a dispute with a client using a larger law firm, if your client has the resources, your firm, using technology and outsourcing, can represent your client just as well as the BigLaw firm can. Even if the other side has the best trial lawyer in the city; you can always engage the best appellate lawyer in the city to handle the appeal! If the parties are engaged in massive discovery, you can always engage third parties to handle the discovery for your client. You can win the large cases.

If your client doesn't have the resources, you can represent your client well by causing the other side the maximum possible discomfort; such that they would rather settle then see you in court again. Target the other side's key weaknesses with precision. Aggressively seek discovery from the other side. Make it clear that you will aggressively cross-examine their executives. You should not ever litigate simply to increase costs on the other side (that is unethical and can backfire), but you can make it clear to the other side that they will have a hell of a fight on their hands if the matter does not settle. Remember the experienced BigLaw partner has been told by the client to make this go away, and they have to answer to the client if the matter can't be resolved quickly and cheaply.

Lesson 5 - try and get the best supervision you can and realize that you won't be perfect

Being a junior lawyer at a SmallLaw firm is often terrifying, but at the same time can be satisfying. The first time you help your clients win a case, buy a house, sell a business is something that you won't get at BigLaw!

The key thing to remember is that you are learning to be a lawyer on the fly, and you will make mistakes. Try and minimize the effect when they happen, but just realize that you can only do your best! The best way to minimize these mistakes is good supervision. Try and make sure you are around senior lawyers (sometimes they may only be a year or two more senior) who you feel comfortable asking questions, asking for precedents and crying on their shoulder. Good supervision will help you learn and become a better lawyer and the better you do at cultivating people who will help you learn, the better a lawyer you will become. Best of luck.

Conclusion

This book is not meant to scare people away from BigLaw or SmallLaw. Rather it is aimed at giving frank realities about life as a junior lawyer and the mistakes that junior lawyers make when they start at a law firm. It is also aimed at busting certain myths about law firm practice, including the necessity of stabbing other junior associates in the back, that any top law firm has only great partners, or that working in SmallLaw is somehow less challenging than BigLaw. Importantly, junior lawyers should realize that just because they have a great law degree from a fancy school they don't need to spend their life doing citation checking, due diligence or discovery, all done in the pursuit of billable hours and eventually partnership. The world of legal practice is richer, more interesting and more satisfying than can ever be perceived by a junior lawyer and, even through the reams of paper (BigLaw) and endless minor contract disputes (SmallLaw) a junior lawyer should be learning, and considering where they want their career to take them.

This book contains very little technical advice, such as research tips, or advocacy tips. This is because, while technical skills are important, law is a profession about communication, diligence and building strong relationships, with colleagues, clients and the community. As a junior lawyer, you are supposed to have technical skills, but what separates the good from the bad junior lawyers are the ones who think about what they are doing, exercise their discretion smartly, and communicate well with their partners and clients. The most successful junior lawyers build relationships, both up with their partners, down with the staff and across the other junior lawyers. You may be in the profession for 40-50 years – you never know whose assistance you will need when, and even if you don't, it is always better to be practicing within a team of people you like and respect.

Finally, other than the few people who would be happy reading cases for 24 hours a day, law is a means to an end: that being a satisfying, fulfilling job that enables you to do some good, provide for your family and make a difference. Never let the demands of the profession get in the way of that realization, and if you have to leave the profession to live a good life, well we're sorry to lose you.

Enjoy the ride!